791·44 PLO

PLOMLEY, R.

Days seemed
longer

£6·95

LAST COPY
If not required by other readers
this item may be renewed, in
person, by post or by telephone.
Please quote details' opposite
and date due for return, If issued
by computer, the numbers on the
barcode label on your ticket and
on each item, together with date
of return are required.

2/1/003/89

9·1·81

Days
Seemed Longer

Days
Seemed Longer

Early Years
of a Broadcaster

Roy Plomley

EYRE METHUEN   LONDON

First published in 1980 by
Eyre Methuen Ltd
11 New Fetter Lane, London EC4P 4EE

Filmset, printed and bound in Great Britain
by Hazell Watson & Viney Ltd,
Aylesbury, Bucks

Plomley, Roy
    Days seemed longer.
    1. Plomley, Roy
    2. Radio broadcasters – Great Britain
    – Biography
    I. Title
    791.44'028'0924   PN1991.4.P/
    ISBN 0-413-39730-0 /471

To Wong

Illustrations

Acknowledgements

I have talked to, or corresponded with, a number of ex-
colleagues in pre-war commercial radio who have kindly
checked facts and figures. They include Stephen Williams,
Jack Hargreaves, OBE, Frank Lamping, Bob Danvers-Walker,
Bernard McNabb, Charles Maxwell, Richard Baines, Norman
Angier, OBE, John Cape, George Carder, 'Sammy' Parker and
Renée Palmer. Bob Danvers-Walker kindly lent a print of the
Radio International photograph, the copyright of which
belongs to Charles Maxwell. I am grateful to them all.

1

As I have discovered by spending leisurely periods of research in Sussex, Somerset and Devon, for the past two hundred years or more my family has been a medical one. Each name that I have turned up has been that of a physician, a surgeon, a surgeon's mate, a surgeon barber, a veterinary surgeon, an apothecary or a toothpuller – so how my obsession by the theatre and all things theatrical came about, I really do not know.

My father, Francis John Plomley, was a pharmaceutical chemist; he was a bald, thickset man with bright blue eyes and a fair beard, and he was the eldest of a family of eleven. It had been his intention to follow in the footsteps of his father, a well-loved physician and surgeon in Maidstone, Kent, but the regular arrival of brothers and sisters – there were nine by the time he left Maidstone Grammar School at the age of 16 – posed financial problems, and he had to accept a more modest and less costly role in the medical world.

For a premium of one hundred and five pounds he was indentured as apprentice to Messrs T. G. and W. B. Stonham, Chemists and Druggists, of Maidstone, for a term of three years and three months 'to learn their art'. On his side, he undertook 'not to commit fornication nor contract matrimony', 'not to play at cards or dice tables' and 'not to haunt taverns and playhouses', while his masters undertook to furnish 'good and sufficient meat drink and lodging' together with 'good and sufficient clothes and washing and mending'. No indication was given of the hours to be worked, but it seemed that it would not be economic for him to spend time and energy walking from and to his home each day – or did the idea that he should live away from home come from his father 'to make a man of him'? – or, perhaps, with the fast-growing family, there just was not room for him. The family lived first at 9 London Road, and later at Knightrider House, which is now the headquarters of the Maidstone and District Omnibus Company.

It was probably after his apprenticeship was completed that he worried his family by embarking on a passionate love affair with a girl cousin, and it had probably been before it that he had got into trouble for jumping his pony over a toll gate to avoid paying the required ha'pence. With his younger brothers, he was noted for occasional roistering in the bars of the Royal Star.

Having qualified as a Member of the Pharmaceutical Society, he took various engagements, including the management of a Maidstone chemist's shop, the owner of which had become insane. In 1895 he went to Cannes to work in the *établissement* Ginner in the rue d'Antibes and, in a lordly manner, took with him the large and comfortable leather-covered armchair which travelled with him from job to job, and in which I am sitting as I write these words. Apparently he did not care for foreign parts, because he stayed in Cannes for only four months and never went abroad again.

It was in 1902, after sojourns in Southampton and in Ilford, that he went into partnership with an oculist named Alldis. They started a business at 51 Fife Road, Kingston-upon-Thames. However, the two partners did not agree and, after only a few years, the business of Plomley and Alldis Ltd became the exclusive concern of my father, while Alldis opened an independent enterprise on the other side of the road.

The photographic trade had been left to Father, the developing, printing and enlarging being carried out in rooms behind the shop. After a while, though, it seemed better to farm this out to a portrait photographer named Newton, who was in business further down the road.

The modest amount of work to be delivered there each day could easily have been transported on a single visit, but my father preferred to make several trips – and if no photographic work had come in, he would take some of his own. The reason for this was his admiration for the receptionist at Newton's, a slim, pretty, dark-haired girl with hazel eyes, whose name was Ellinor Maud Wigg. She was twelve years younger than my father, and she spoke with a slight but attractive southern American drawl, because she had spent twelve years of her childhood in New Orleans, Louisiana.

She was a Norfolk girl, the daughter of a former agricultural engineer named Wright Heyhoe Wigg, who wore luxuriant whiskers and brightly-coloured waistcoats. With his wife Caroline, his two young children, Percy and Maud, and a grey parrot in a cage, he had set off for the New World in 1885 on the SS *Paris*, bound from Antwerp to New Orleans, proposing to travel overland to California.

Mechanical breakdowns lengthened the voyage to five weeks and stretched financial resources to breaking point, so the journey to California was abandoned and the family settled in New Orleans. They took lodgings in Algiers, on the opposite bank of the Mississippi to the city. My grandfather accepted the first job that was offered him, as an engineer on a river boat. In the tropical heat, this was gruelling, and he claimed that he never worked harder than for his first silver dollar, which he had mounted as a brooch for Caroline to treasure and wear.

Better times were to come, and after a brief spell as a city fireman, he became chief engineer on a sugar plantation, finally settling down in the advertisement department of the daily newspaper, the *Times-Picayune*. He was happy working among newspaper people because he had a literary bent himself, and had kept a detailed and amusing journal of the long voyage from England.

From Algiers, the family moved across the river to Elysian

Fields, then to a first-floor apartment in St Peter Street, in the old French quarter where almost every house displayed a tracery of wrought iron, and finally they moved uptown to a house in Carrolton, under the levee. As my grandfather had spent two years as a student in Germany, he decided to send Percy and Maud to a German Lutheran school where no English was spoken, even in the playground.

When school was over, they pulled off their shoes and stockings and played barefoot with children of every nationality. They roamed the levees, swam, joined in guerrilla warfare against gangs of negro children – my mother had a small round scar on her face caused by the spout of a well-aimed coffee-pot seized from a rubbish heap – and, on one occasion, dragged home a dead alligator to skin it for its hide. They had instructions to avoid any house where a yellow flag was flying, because that meant fever. Sanitation on the outskirts of the city was primitive, and before drinking a glass of water one waited for innumerable organisms to sink to the bottom. Seemingly inoculated against everything, it is not surprising that both Percy and Maud enjoyed good health until their mid-eighties.

In due course, Percy joined his father on the *Times-Picayune* as a junior reporter. As befitted his age, he started with flower-shows and inquests, but for senior newsgetters they were lively days: lynchings were frequent, and the press were sometimes notified in advance, so that a representative might be sent. One afternoon, a mob had dragged eleven members of the Mafia from the jail and shot or hanged them all, an incident which had nearly involved the United States in war with Italy.

There were many perquisites from the newspaper, including weekly theatre tickets, with opportunities to see Irving and Bernhardt, and steamship excursions up the Mississippi to cruise among the overhanging mosses of the bayous.

After twelve years, my grandmother's tendency to asthma had been aggravated so much by the climate that it was decided to return to England. The family travelled by sea to New York, where they spent a week sightseeing, and then sailed to Glasgow in the SS *Circassia*, a converted private yacht. The crossing was made in the comparative comfort of the second cabin class, and the fare was thirty-five dollars a head. They still had the grey parrot, a surly bird which was to continue to peck all comers for another thirty years, and smuggled over a small terrier named Tip, for which they did not buy a ticket.

They rented a cottage overlooking the royal paddocks in the Thameside village of Hampton Wick, and my grandfather became advertisement representative for a monthly magazine circulating in Surrey. Percy decided that he wanted to become an electrical engineer, and Maud, fired by an American sense of independence, announced that she too was going to work, which was not what was expected of a well-brought-up English girl of sixteen. She found employment at Hill's, a china and glass shop in Brighton Road, Surbiton, and walked more than two miles there and back each day, putting in long hours for fourteen shillings a month. In due course, she was entrusted with buying stock, and made frequent trips to City warehouses. Then, for a while, she worked in the chinaware department of the Bon Marché in Brixton, before taking the job as photographer's receptionist where she met my father. She sometimes appeared in PSA concerts at the St James's Hall, Kingston, reciting 'Asleep at the Switch' or 'The Man with One Hair'.

She was engaged to a young man named Harry Taylor, but the engagement lasted seven years, which seems to indicate a doubt in the mind of one of the parties. We may assume that party to have been my mother, because she sent Harry packing and exchanged his ring on the second finger of her left hand for another, with twelve small diamonds surrounding a ruby, offered by my father.

The wedding was at St John's Church, Hampton Wick, with a reception at the nearby Assembly Rooms. The bride wore soft white silk and carried a shower bouquet of lilies of the valley and white roses. The honeymoon was spent at Eastbourne.

A neat little semi-detached house was rented in King's Road, Kingston, a rather characterless road which stretches from

Lower Ham Road, past the barracks of what was then the East Surrey Regiment, to the gate of Richmond Park. They called the house Oxshott, because of their many cycle excursions to Oxshott woods during their courtship. Their combined bank balance at the time of their marriage was eighty-six pounds, and my father drew four pounds a week from the business. On this they could manage quite well. Later, however, it seemed more expedient to live in the two-storeyed flat above the shop in Fife Road, where I was born in the top front room. I was an only child, my mother having previously given birth to two premature and stillborn sons, so, as can be imagined, my safe arrival as a lusty, bawling, living infant was greeted with joy. My father was already 45.

A chemist's shop is a fascinating place to a child. I liked the sweet, musky smell that greeted me every time I pushed open the door, heavy with a glass-covered advertisement for eau de Cologne, which divided our living quarters from the shop. Next to that door was a glass-fronted cupboard full of sponges, with a layer of real sand from the sea covering the bottom.

To go out to the street one had to pass through the shop, and it was always interesting to see who was standing at the counter or sitting on the two bentwood chairs, which were provided for those who were frail or who had to wait for a prescription. Sometimes, when the shop was full, one had to push one's way through. Just by the door was a tall looking-glass, in which I watched myself grow up. When we left Kingston — I was 20 then — I asked for that looking-glass as my own souvenir of 51 Fife Road.

From eight in the morning until eight in the evening, and much later on Saturdays, there was movement and activity; the broken rhythm of footsteps, the clang of the cash register, the clink of bottles, the whirring of pestle in mortar, the clonk as the brass trays of the balance hit the base. Every morning, delivery men clumped along the passage to the stock room, carrying big brown cardboard boxes full of remedies for coughs and colds and constipation, or expensively wrapped cosmetics, all to be unpacked and ranged neatly on shelves or in drawers or cupboards. Sometimes, goods arrived in wooden packing cases which were wrenched open with a jemmy, and the contents lifted out of a sweet-smelling nest of straw. There was a mysterious cupboard, crammed with blue and green bottles each with a label reading 'Poison', which was to be opened only by my father, and there was a cellar which smelt of coal dust, with a passage lined with shelves of empty bottles of a myriad sizes and shapes.

I explored in secret the contents of the serried, shiny, glass-handled drawers with labels in abbreviated Latin. In the dispensary was a drawer full of mysteries, which became only semi-mysteries as I began to have an idea of how life is planned: there were pessaries and Dutch caps and neat little packets of French letters. One economical model of the last was made of thick rubber, to be washed and reused until it wore out, and was called 'The Workman's Friend'.

The number of assistants engaged by my father fluctuated with the state of trade. Some of the time there was only Mr Browning, a red-faced man who always wore a blue suit and a neat regimental tie, who had to go after a regrettable incident when, looking after the premises while the family was on holiday, he gave a wild party and left the place in a terrible mess. During a brief period of prosperity there were three, two men and a woman, and there was always an errand boy, who came after school to replenish the coal scuttles and deliver prescriptions from a black, shiny satchel. Each purchase, however small, was neatly wrapped in white paper and tied with thin red string or sealed with red wax, for which purpose a gas jet was kept burning behind the counter.

The household was completed by a daily help, who swept and washed the shop floor while we were at breakfast, then came upstairs to help with the housework, wait at table for our midday meal, and take me for a walk in the afternoon. There was a dear, bright girl named May Penny, who was with us for years, and she was succeeded by Phyllis Spreadbury, who is my friend still.

We lived comfortably, if frugally, and new clothes were a

17

treat. When necessary, my father went to a tailor named Ellisdon, in Thames Street, and ordered a suit; it was supplied with two pairs of trousers and, although the pattern of the dark, serviceable cloth varied slightly from suit to suit, the style was always that of a few years before the Great War, with the jacket buttoned high on the chest. He wore boots rather than shoes, because they gave him more support for a job in which he was standing most of the day. Mother took an interest in fashion, although she never pursued the ephemeral, because clothes had to last. Her ordinary wear was a smart two-piece, with a jumper which she had crocheted herself. She had never learned to knit but she crocheted beautifully, and she had a drawer full of tablecloths on which she had worked with immense patience, and which were brought out on high days and holidays. Most of the furniture in our flat was solid and serviceable, and much of it had been acquired at the second-hand auction sales held by A. G. Bonsor & Co. Ltd, whose offices and saleroom were immediately opposite.

Our dining-room, which was also our sitting-room, was in the front on the first floor. Outside the window, over the front section of the shop, were 'the leads', where lead sheeting waterproofed the roof of a later extension. It would have needed only a very modest amount of rebuilding to convert one of the windows into a glass door and turn the leads into a balcony, but none of the owners of the ten shops which formed the terrace had done so – and none of them has done so to this day.

My parents had their armchairs on either side of the fireplace, which was on the right as one entered the room. My father's chair, which was the one he had taken to the south of France, had its back to the window; my mother's was smaller and it had a straighter back, because she liked to sit upright. In the bay on her right was a desk with bookshelves beneath it. The books included a German Bible and the complete works of Tennyson (in fact, two copies of the complete works of Tennyson, because a second one had been presented by Sir Harry Brittain as a gesture of thanks to my parents for their kindness to a lady who had been taken ill while being driven through Kingston in his car), the complete works of Shakespeare, bound in squashy red but in such small print as to be useless, a treatise on how perfumes were made, doubtless presented to Father on some trade occasion, and another on how to make paper flowers, a history of Louisiana, a novel by Sir Walter Scott which was a school prize of Mother's, *Pears' Encyclopedia*, *Sixty Years a Queen*, volumes of verse by Mrs Hemans and Owen Meredith, and a few novels. Above the desk hung a large framed photograph of Mother and Father on their wedding day. Beside my father's chair was a small table with a shelf for newspapers and books and, on the other side, a smoker's table, with a rack for pipes and a wooden tobacco jar. On the wall in the bay on his side was a photograph of his father. On the chimney piece was a heavy black pillared clock and some vases. Above hung a looking glass and two coloured bas-reliefs, of the Porta Nigra, in Trier, and the Arco di Constantino, in Rome.

In the centre of the room was a circular dining table, which had an extra leaf to be inserted when necessary, and it was covered by a brown cloth with a fringe. Round it stood four upholstered dining chairs. When the room was being cleaned, the four chairs were stood in line in the passage outside, and they made a very satisfactory tunnel for me to crawl through. Along the inside wall was a settee, with ends which let down to turn it into a spare bed.

By the side wall near the door was an oak sideboard with sharp corners, to which a scar on my forehead attests to this day. On it were two biscuit barrels, a tantalus with cut-glass bottles for whisky and gin, a fruit bowl and a silver crumb scoop with a horn handle. On small shelves were postcard-size photographs of my two grandmothers.

For some years, in the bay by Father's armchair, there was a sparrow in a cage. He was called Tinker, and he had been found with a broken wing when very young. He took to cage life very well and chirped away happily, going into paroxysms of joy when he heard the lid of a biscuit barrel rattled. When he died, he was replaced by a succession of canaries, of the Hartz Mountain Roller variety.

When I was very young, we had a black and brown mongrel named Moses, who had been brought from King's Road. I have been told that he guarded my cradle most faithfully and permitted no unauthorized person to approach. One of my very earliest memories is of crawling under the dining table to give him food.

Two large sentimental engravings hung on the wall above the settee, one of them called 'Her First Love Letter', and between the windows was a large photograph of a leafy Surrey lane. By the door was a Kingston scene, with early Victorian Derby Day traffic splashing through the Hogg's Mill Stream. Outside the door was a butler's tray, set on a folding frame, on which dishes were placed on their way from the kitchen.

The lighting was by gas, of course, which gave a brave white light, hissing out of fragile white mantles which were bought in green cardboard boxes. A match was lit, one of a pair of chains hanging down from the shade was pulled gently, and the match applied to the mantle. There was a pleasant little pop and the light hissed into being.

The back room on the first floor was the drawing-room, which was used only for Mother's cards afternoons and for my birthday parties. It smelled of pot-pourri and was furnished mainly with Japanese pieces inlaid with mother-of-pearl. On the walls were marine watercolours, and on a table was an *art nouveau* figure in green plaster of a nude girl holding up a crescent moon into which a circular looking-glass was fitted.

The kitchen, at the very back, was rather crowded, because it contained, side-by-side, both a blackleaded range and a gas stove, and there was a heavy mangle which folded into a table when not in use. There was no room in the flat for a separate bathroom, so the bath was in the kitchen, hidden by a flap which could be lifted and hooked against the wall. The window looked out onto an orchard which belonged to the London and South Western Railway Company, the fruit being one of the perquisites of the stationmaster. On the top floor, there were two bedrooms.

It was while coming down the stairs from the top floor that I levitated, on two occasions. I do not know how old I was – three or four, I suppose – and I remember it very vividly. At the top of the staircase, my feet lifted, and I floated gently down with my heels just an inch or two above the edges of the treads. My hand was on the smooth banister rail, and I remember looking at a steel engraving which hung on the passage wall as I floated downwards past it. It was called 'Little Lady Bountiful', and it showed the young daughter of rich parents taking a tray of luxury foods to some ragged boys who were fishing, while the proud picnicking parents beamed in the background.

The sensation was delightful and I was not in the least alarmed. I remember running into the kitchen to tell Mother about it, and I have no doubt that her response would have been a tolerant and reassuring, 'Did you, dear?'. The two occasions were close together, and the experiences were identical. Child psychologists will doubtless have a rational explanation, but I will swear on as big a stack of Bibles as can be assembled that I have been twice lifted gently off this earth.

As I believe is common with an only child, I invented a companion. His name was Harry and he went with me everywhere. I would not go for a walk unless Harry was coming; I would not eat up my food until I was assured that Harry had eaten his; I would not clean my teeth unless Harry was at the same task. I have no idea how long the game lasted, but Harry was a great comfort to me and I am sure he fulfilled a need.

Mother was very houseproud, and everything was polished until it shone. Her particular loves were the bits and pieces of china and cut glass which she collected and about which, of course, she was knowledgeable. In her youth, she had been very pretty indeed, and I have a photograph of her, aged 15, as the Vain Queen in a church young people's production of 'Snowdrop and the Seven Dwarves' in New Orleans, which is enchanting.

My father was a quiet, gentle person, always considerate, always courteous. Having worked cruelly long hours ever since he had started his apprenticeship, he had acquired few social accomplishments; he had never learned to play tennis, nor was he interested in bridge or billiards or clubs: at the end of the day, he was ready for his armchair and his slippers and his pipe. This restricted my mother's social life to the daytime, and there was a constant series of tea parties for which each member of her circle of friends took it in turns to be hostess. When it was Mother's turn, sixteen or twenty chattering females were crammed into our tiny drawing-room for a game of rummy or cooncan.

I can remember my parents having only one quarrel. I do not know what it was about, and its only manifestation was an aloofness that lasted just a few hours. I went into their bedroom to say goodnight and, to my astonishment, they were not speaking to each other. I made some jocular remark, which was greeted rather stonily, and the next day the whole thing had been forgotten.

The morning shopping expedition with Mother was a high spot of my infant day. The big general store, Bentalls, was exciting to visit, especially the drapery department, with its morning-coated floorwalkers ready with a pair of scissors to snip a sample from a bolt of material at the request of an undecided shopper, and the toy department in the basement was a wonderland, especially on days when the river was running high and water oozed up through the parquet floor. Mother said she remembered Bentalls, when she had returned from America in the late nineties, as a modest-sized drapers, although it was hard to envisage. The store had, in fact, been established in the 1860s and, by progressively forcing out a neighbouring school, a mission house, a vicarage and a slaughter house, it had grown and grown and was still growing. It even acquired an entrance in Fife Road and, to Father's disgust, the then head of the firm, Leonard H. Bentall, was reputed to have announced 'I'm going to kill Fife Road', a vainglorious boast which, I am glad to say, he never succeeded in fulfilling.

The expensive toys in Bentalls basement were to be dreamed of only when Christmas or a birthday approached. But Mother would often buy me the more modest playthings vended in the street; there were paper windmills on sticks – the faster one ran, the faster they would whirl round; there were wavers, consisting of a cardboard tube with a bunch of coloured streamers at the end, and a cock-a-doodle-doo toy, which was a fluffy chicken's head from which hung a length of waxed string, down which one jerked thumb and forefinger to produce either a cock's crow or a hen's clucks.

At Marks and Spencer's – the open-fronted Penny Bazaar – tin toys were on sale at a penny, as well as hundreds of useful household articles at the same price. I remember a day when Woolworth's was selling a special line in galvanized iron buckets for sixpence, and it seemed as if every man, woman and child in the town was carrying home one of these bargains.

Sometimes I would be taken into Lyons teashop in Thames Street for an ice-cream soda, which was delicious and a great luxury. It seemed to me that one of the blessings of being grown-up must be to carry money in one's pocket or handbag, and be able to stroll in to order an ice-cream soda whenever one felt like it. I think they were fivepence, which was quite a lot of money, and I was sometimes limited to a phosphate, which was a brightly-coloured fizzy drink which cost only twopence. There was no self-service in the twenties. One sat on a bentwood chair at a glass-topped table and waited for one of the 'nippies', who wore black frocks and frilly white caps and aprons, to take the order. Waiting was no hardship because there was the menu to read. It was large, four pages printed on yellow card, and when you had savoured, in imagination, the steak-and-kidney pudding (7d) and chipped potatoes (3d) there was the fascinating back page, which was a miniature magazine with articles on sport and travel.

In some of the drapery stores, an overhead change-giving system was used, with metal cylinders whooshing along stout wires to the back of the shop, from whence they would be returned in the same way, thumping into metal baskets, where they would be opened and the change given to the shopper, wrapped in the bill. Most fabrics were priced at just under the nearest shilling – at two shillings and elevenpence threefarthings, for example – and one could choose, instead of the farthing change, to have an array of pins, neatly stuck into a roll of pink paper.

Another shop I enjoyed visiting was Follett's, the pork butchers in the Market Place, where there was thick sawdust on the floor and a fabulous display of sausages and hams and trotters and pâtés and delicious quivering brawns. It was outside Follett's that I once saw a man who had collapsed in the street being pushed off to hospital in a hand ambulance, a twowheeled vehicle like an elongated pram.

My personal shopping was mainly conducted at a tiny sweet and toy shop in Richmond Road, just behind the station. It was originally called Thompson's and was kept by an elderly lady in black, until it changed hands and was called Langdon and Phillips. That was rather a mouthful to say but presumably proclaimed the identities of two middle-aged ladies, who were very cheerful and nice, although how there could have been a living for two I cannot understand, because nothing in the shop seemed to cost more than a penny or two.

Fife Road is about a quarter of a mile long, and it runs in an S-bend from the railway station to Clarence Street, which is the main shopping thoroughfare. It consisted almost entirely of small, privately-owned shops, interspersed with a few houses. At the station end was the Kingston Hotel, which was large and solid, and further down was a small restaurant and a Temperance Billiard Hall.

Of course, there were characters: there was little Mr Sparrow, who doubled as newsagent and watch repairer, and who was always in shirtsleeves, with a cigarette dangling from his lower lip. Every few months, my grandfather would look in to ask about his gold watch, which he had taken in to be repaired some years before, but Mr Sparrow always said that it wasn't ready yet. Eventually my grandfather stopped asking, surmising that Mr Sparrow had either lost it, or sold it during some crisis which had contributed to his permanent air of depression. Then there was old Mr Wheeler, who was very old indeed, and who moved slowly up and down the road, white-whiskered and leaning over his stick. Once, while out with my mother, I had been bidden 'Shake hands with Mr Wheeler', and my childish but firm handshake had been enough to put him off his balance, and Mother had to help him up and dust him down. And there were the Nightingale brothers, both bearded and jolly, who kept adjoining tobacconist shops, one retail and one wholesale. Sometimes when I went in on an errand for my father to buy an ounce of Bond of Union, one of them would conspiratorially slip back a copper or two to me.

Being a busy street with little through traffic, we were much favoured by street musicians. Barrel organists were frequent visitors, and so was a sad-faced man who played sad tunes on a one-stringed fiddle. Sometimes a Punch and Judy man would perform, but that would be at the bottom of the road, near Clarence Street.

There can be few places within twelve miles of the centre of London which have more attractions than Kingston-upon-Thames. My favourite afternoon excursion was to the riverside Canbury Gardens where, suddenly, at the age of four – or was it five? – I discovered that I could read. Then there is Richmond Park, Charles I's great 2,000-acre hunting enclosure, with hills, streams and noble trees, and great tracts of bracken into which a small child can disappear. Just across the river are Bushey Park and Home Park, the twin parks of Hampton Court, and the gardens and courtyards of the ancient palace itself. The town still had a rural air: on Monday mornings, the farmers of Tolworth and the Dittons drove their cattle, sheep and pigs into the Market Place, where they were herded into whitewashed pens. In the shops and on the market stalls were mountains of fresh farm produce, fruit and vegetables which tasted of the earth and not of chemicals. The scene was brightly coloured and very English; one turned to stare at the owner of a foreign voice, and the only dark skins were on the faces of gipsies.

It was the construction of the bypass in the late twenties that led to the surburban sprawl which now links the Royal Borough with the London conurbation. The town itself, choked with traffic, has become industrial, and a shopping centre for East Surrey. Fife Road has acquired a raucous air: the houses have gone, the small businesses have been replaced by branches of multiple firms, there are parking meters down both sides, and there is a pervading smell from the premises of purveyors of takeaway hamburgers and kebabs.

One of the drawbacks of living right in the centre of the town was that, although the bustle was enjoyable, there were so few children immediately at hand to play with. There were the children of Owen Thomas, the draper, opposite, but they were a large family and they seemed to form a self-contained group. When I was very young, my playmates were Gwen and Betty, the daughters of Mrs Phillips, who sold handbags in the front half of No. 47, and Mr Phillips, who dressed gentlemen's hair in the back half, and for a while there was a little girl named Alice who lived upstairs at No. 53. One day, she confided to me that she knew how boys went wee-wee, and I looked at her, mystified, for obviously there was only one way for anyone to go wee-wee. Disappointingly, she added no further information. The fact that her parents were Belgian must have been responsible for her outrageous conversation.

In my virtual solitude I read, voraciously, everything that came to hand. My parents subscribed to two monthly magazines, *The Premier* and *Twenty Story* and, later, they belonged to W. H. Smith & Son's library, but the two main sources of my literary education were the bookstall inside the railway station and a secondhand bookshop in Fife Road kept by Messrs Cooper, who were father and son. In the station, I would spend hours examining the array of brightly-covered weekly and monthly periodicals displayed on trestle tables. Occasionally, when the manager was not looking, I would take a quick skim through the pages of one of them, but the rules of the game were that, unless a purchase of some sort was planned, you could look but not touch. With the Coopers,

26

things were different. Their shop was open-fronted, and they both held a tolerant view of the browser, presumably because nobody expected their stock to be free of fingermarks. There were few books displayed in the Cooper frontage which went unbrowsed by me, although I was hardly ever a customer because my parents insisted that to bring secondhand books of unknown provenance into the house was to risk scarlet fever and other fearsome diseases. In fact, during my early school-days I remember being allowed to bring home only one book from Coopers, and that was a history book which could have been useful to me for an exam. It was baked in the oven before I was allowed to read it. Why it was more dangerous to read such books at home than it was while standing at Messrs Coopers' frontage I do not know, unless it was felt that the risk of contagion was less in the open air.

The same prejudice put paid to any suggestion that I should join the public library; whereas books from the W. H. Smith library were all right because the borrowers subscribed, and were therefore people of substance and less likely to spread infection. This was consistent with the fact that I was not allowed to venture into whole areas of Kingston, because the inhabitants were classed as slum-dwellers.

I was a dedicated reader of the school stories by the incredibly prolific Charles Hamilton, who wrote, under different names, the Greyfriars stories for *The Magnet*, the St Jim's stories for *The Gem* and the Rookwood stories for *The Boy's Friend*, and I also absorbed as many of the adventures of Sexton Blake as I could lay hands on, especially those featuring the dastardly villain, Zenith the Albino. A little gentle censorship was exercised by my father, although he passed most of the publications of the Amalgamated Press. There were ways round the various bannings, of course: I was not allowed to read *Dracula*, but I discovered that it was being serialized in *Argosy*, and there was no ban on reading that.

I was so fascinated by the Greyfriars stories that, at the age of seven, I wrote to Harry Wharton, leader of the Famous Five, and asked them all to tea. They were to bring Billy

Bunter as well. The reply came from the editor of *The Magnet*. 'Many thanks for your jolly letter to Harry Wharton,' he wrote, '. . . and am only sorry that I have to disappoint you by replying to your note myself. There is really no other way. Harry Wharton is a character in the yarns, and he cannot very well deal with correspondence outside of Greyfriars.' I like the way he put that: he was careful not to disillusion his young reader by saying, in so many words, that Harry Wharton did not exist. 'I hope your interest in the Companion Papers will continue. You are a grand supporter, and your offer to entertain Bunter himself shows first class generosity. The Owl is a simple terror at a teaparty.' He concluded his letter by telling me the publication date of the next *Holiday Annual*, and adding that he had 'an extremely interesting new feature starting shortly in *The Magnet*'.

Later I began to collect the hardback volumes of The Readers Library, which were sold in Woolworth's, bound in red and gold with a coloured dustjacket, at only sixpence each. Here were the works of Dickens and Dumas and H. G. Wells and Rider Haggard at a really knockdown price, even if the binding was of unfolded sheets and the glue broke apart at the first rough handling.

Another Woolworth bargain was the variety of surplus copies of American pulp magazines, shipped over in ballast and sold at threepence. Some of the stuff was rubbish, but the Street and Smith publications, such as *Western Story Magazine* and *Detective Story Magazine* were always worth reading, and so was *Black Mask*, which gave a pre-talking-picture insight into gang warfare and other less attractive aspects of life in the USA.

It was in one of those pulps that I came across a story which made a great impression on me. Who the author was, I have no idea, and I can remember few details. It was a fantasy, which began in the New York apartment of a distinguished writer who was an authority on eighteenth-century London. As a reward for a service undertaken for a supernatural being, he was offered a single hour in which he might observe at first hand the life of the past, and he chose an hour sitting in the Cheshire Cheese, listening to Dr Samuel Johnson, his idol, talking with his cronies. He had to promise that during his precious sixty minutes he would sit quietly and not utter a single word.

The magic was worked, and there he was in the smoky old pub. Johnson was sitting in an opposite corner with Garrick, Reynolds, Goldsmith, Wilkes and Boswell, and the doctor was in top form.

Just before the hour was up, Johnson got up to go, being handed his coat, hat, stick and gloves by a waiter. Bidding his friends good night, the great man pushed his way through the company to the door, dropping one of his gloves at the writer's feet. The temptation was too strong: he leaned forward, picked up the glove and held it out to the retreating Johnson. 'Your glove, doctor,' he called. Johnson turned and took it, with a growled 'Thank 'ee, sir,' and went out into the night.

Within a few moments, the writer found himself back in New York — but instead of being in his book-lined apartment in the East-Sixties, he was at the bottom of a huge crater, surrounded by putrefaction and rubble. He shouted for help, and the supernatural being appeared, shaking his head worriedly. 'You promised not to say a word, and now look what you've done. I don't see how we're going to remedy this.'

'I gave him his glove, that's all.'

'And as a result his coach reached the corner of the street three seconds later than it should have done, and it collided with another coach in which was a pregnant woman. The shock of the collision caused her to miscarry, and a child who would have grown into a great soldier was not born. Because Britain did not have the services of that man at Waterloo, the battle was lost, a power-drunk Napoleon and his successors set out to conquer the world, warfare continued for a century, and more and more powerful weapons were developed. In August 1910, a devastating new explosive was launched against New York, and the city no longer exists. You see the damage that a few words can do.'

While writing this book, and looking back at so many incidents I remember, I have been conscious that words or actions of mine have changed the story not only for myself but for many others. To live is a great responsibility.

We were occasional patrons of the Kingston Empire, the back of which we could see from our windows. Father would book three seats in the dress circle for the first house on Wednesday, which was early closing day, and I remember seeing the mystifying Great Carmo, and Harry and Burton Lester and their cowboy show, and *Splinters*, the ex-army company which was full of female impersonators, and hundreds of acrobats, jugglers and ventriloquists whose skill was admired but whose names were forgotten as soon as the following week's bills were posted up.

Father used to get bored during musical acts, because he was one of the only two men I have known who were tone deaf. He was quite unable to hear a tune, and used to go about the house humming little rhythms on one note.

As a result of his inevitable lack of interest, we had no piano, although there was a hand-wound gramophone with two or three dozen records which were kept, upright, in a box covered with black velvet. They were a mixed batch, and included a few music-hall performers such as Harry Lauder and Billy Williams, a version of the ageless 'Cohen on the Telephone', some military band and orchestral pieces, two or three wartime patriotic records, including *The Landing of the British in France*, a number of discs which catered for Mother's Louisiana memories, with such titles as *Down among the Sugar Cane* and *Plantation Pastimes*, some operatic items, mainly orchestral but with a couple of arias from *Maritana* and *The Bohemian Girl*, and quite a collection of ballads, mostly sung by tenors, including 'In an Old-Fashioned Town', 'I Hear You Calling Me' and 'Just Because the Violets'. The only piece of 'classical' music was Bach's Fugue in D minor played on the organ, and a centre-piece was an album set of *Indian Love Lyrics*, on four single-sided discs. The gramophone was seldom played but occasionally, after I was in bed, I would hear the music coming up the stairs. In due course, I began adding to the collection myself, contributing mainly popular dance tunes and musical comedy excerpts.

Sometimes we would go to one of Kingston's four cinemas. Our favourite was the Super, which was in Fife Road, and which had started life as the County Theatre. It had a charming rounded auditorium, with golden cherubs on the front of the boxes, and clusters of pink-shaded lights which dimmed down slowly and excitingly before the programme began. The best seats were in the circle and were one and threepence; the back stalls were ninepence, and the front stalls fivepence. It was one of the few cinemas in which the projection was from behind the screen.

I had heard a lot about 'the pictures' when I was very young, from May Penny, and I was eager to see this marvel. One day she told me she had seen the next week's pictures being carried into the Super, and I had a mental picture of two men carrying over their shoulders some red embroidered banners. I think I had got this idea from the Salvation Army, who used to parade down Fife Road every Sunday with band playing and banners flying. Eventually, at the age of five, I was taken to the Super Cinema, and I saw a film about a motor race, during which one of the drivers was tied to a post to stop him competing. Soon I became a regular patron and used to follow the fifteen-instalment serials. The best of these were *The Lost City*, in which I remember an intrepid explorer being enlaced by a man-eating tree, and *Hurricane Hutch*, in which an actor named Charles Hutchinson performed daring feats on trains, motorcycles, and all other forms of mechanical transport.

Other cinemas were the Elite, which was new and rather grand, with a pillared entrance and a tea lounge with basket chairs, and the Kinema, which was a long shed-like building with very little atmosphere.

All three boasted a small orchestra to accompany the films, but the fourth had only a piano. That was the Cinem Palace, which was the least comfortable and the most down-market, with a twice-weekly change of programme. Although the other cinemas plastered the district with big, garish, brightly-coloured pictorial posters, the Cinem Palace confined itself to plain double-crown bills printed in black on yellow paper. They gave a minimum of information, and a typical half-week's programme would read:

'THE DESERT OUTLAW'
Drama in 7 parts. B. JONES and E. BRENT

'SURGING SEAS'
Drama in 6 parts. C. HUTCHINSON and E. THORNTON

'BATTLING BREWSTER'
Episode 12, in 2 parts. F. FARNUM

plus News and Comedy.

'Parts' referred to the number of reels.

The pianist was housed in an elevated box fixed to the wall at the side of the screen, and he climbed to it up a ladder. His eyeline could have given him only a hazy idea of what the film was about, but he did his best, switching from dramatic *agitato* to Chopin and then to a current dance tune, and it is to his efforts that I owe most of what slight knowledge I have of the piano repertoire.

I went to the Cinem Palace quite frequently, usually on my own on Saturday afternoons, and the management specialized in good westerns. At the end of the performance, I would come out blinking in the daylight, and walking with the stiff bow-legged gait of an avenging cowboy. I enjoyed all films, even society dramas, because to a child there is no such thing as a bad film, merely films which have dull patches.

One facet of cinema-going which is no longer encountered is the ritual squirting: at least once during every performance, an attendant would pass down the aisles squirting a highly-scented liquid into the air. Whether its purpose was to disinfect the audience or deodorize the cinema I have never found out.

Films stimulated my already vivid imagination and, apart from the personal fantasies which I spun for myself, I evolved fast-moving adventures for my toys. My lead soldiers never fought battles but escaped down pieces of string from danger on the dizzy heights of the chimneypiece, fought mountainous waves in the bath, which made their bright paint fade, or emerged unscathed from the train wrecks which, as I had no mechanical interests at all, were the only use to which I put my Hornby train set.

I saw two films in production. Once, while on an afternoon walk with May Penny, we crossed Kingston Bridge to Hampton Wick, presumably bound for one of the royal parks, and saw a crowd outside one of the houses at the bridge foot. A man was turning the handle of a hand-cranked camera, and an actor and actress were playing a scene on the steps of the house. 'It's Henry Edwards and Chrissie White!' exclaimed May excitedly. The names meant nothing to me, but they were among the most popular stars of the day.

The second occasion was several years later, when a film unit set up outside the railway station, and a number of young actors, their faces covered with bright yellow make-up, were observed nipping in and out of the Kingston Hotel. It was a film about the popular comedy character, Bindle, who was a furniture removal man, and Kingston station was taking the place of Oxford station, which apparently it then resembled.

Very few of the films I remember from childhood were British, although there was a most exciting highwayman drama, *Dick Turpin's Ride to York*, starring Matheson Lang, with a very sad scene when gallant Black Bess collapsed and died at the very gates of the city, and there was *Three Men in a Boat*, which had local interest because the three men were shown looking at Kingston's Coronation Stone – and there were the war films, *Zebrugge*, *Ypres* and *The Retreat from Mons*, which were spectacular reconstructions of British actions. Some of the trench warfare scenes had been shot in nearby Surbiton.

The many westerns I saw have blurred together – although I recall the stars with affection, particularly Tom Mix and

Buck Jones and the baby-faced Hoot Gibson — and I can remember some of the epics, such as *The Covered Wagon* and *The Iron Horse*. There were some good pirate films, too, especially *The Black Pirate*, the first Technicolour production, with Douglas Fairbanks and a wonderfully inventive underwater battle, which was copied forty years later in a James Bond film. There was *Captain Blood*, too, and *The Sea Hawk*, with Milton Sills. Other memorable spectacles included the biblical epics, *Ben Hur*, *The Ten Commandments* and *Moon of Israel*, which included an unbelievable shot of an axe cleaving into a man's bare back during a battle — and to this day I don't know how they faked that.

I wanted to see *The Lost World* so much that when, at last, I was sitting in the Super Cinema and the lights were going down I just could not believe my good fortune. Taken from Conan Doyle's adventure novel, the trick effects of prehistoric animals were something that the cinema had never before achieved.

Many of the films were released in tinted copies, with night sequences tinted blue, sunlight sequences yellow — and, if there was a fire, the screen went red. There was a very exciting animal film called *Chang*, in which the climax was an elephant stampede. Before this sequence, an announcement appeared on the screen asking for the indulgence of the audience while technical changes were made. We sat in the darkness for a minute or so and then, wonder of wonders, the screen grew before our eyes to three times its normal size, and the elephants appeared to be trampling the cinema flat. Had we known it, we were watching a preview of the anomorphic lenses which were to be used twenty-five years later for various big-screen systems.

I had no clear idea as to who was my favourite comedian. Perhaps it was Harold Lloyd, because he had a timidity which I could well understand, and his character was middle-class, which made him easier to identify with than the low-life characterizations of Charlie Chaplin and Harry Langdon.

When my age passed into double figures, I began to take a

34

healthy interest in some of the younger and livelier actresses. I favoured those who played comedy, of course; I could not be doing with the vamps and tragediennes. Colleen Moore I liked, and Clara Bow, and the gorgeous Janet Gaynor. I always tried to see college comedies, because in those the characters went about in a high-spirited gang and I longed to be part of a gang.

Quite a number of Continental films were shown, although they were not billed as such. An exception was Henri Fescourt's *Les Miserables*, which was spread over two weeks and which I went to see with a school party; and there was *Metropolis*, which made the most of its German modernism. Most of the others needed a little guess-work to decide where they had been made, although there was often a clue in a street name or a newpaper headline. If the hero was pasty-faced and a stone or two overweight, it was a fair guess that the film was German.

The short films were interesting, too. I enjoyed the Felix the Cat cartoons, and there was an ingenious half-animation half-live-action series called *Out of the Inkwell*, in which cartoons were drawn and brought to life before your eyes. Occasionally there would be a colour short, lasting just a minute or so, in which each frame had been laboriously coloured by hand. I remember hand-colouring being used to considerable effect in a film version of the famous farce, *Alf's Button*: when Alf unwisely said, 'Strike me pink!' he really did go that colour.

We usually took our summer holiday at the beginning of September when, although the days are shorter, the crowds have gone. During the more prosperous years, we went away for a few days in the spring as well, and in one especially good year we took a girl named Annie with us, just to look after me. We usually went to Eastbourne or Brighton, although in earlier days we had been fond of Cliftonville. Once we went to Bognor, which was just a little too quiet, and once to Bournemouth, where it rained all the time, so we cut our losses and came home several days early.

Sometimes Father would hire a car to transport us and our

luggage. On one occasion, our driver was a civil young man, with a moustache and a cloth cap, who nodded understandingly when told that we would enjoy seeing the countryside and would like him to take his time. Some years later, we became accustomed to seeing his photograph in the newspapers, because his name was Kaye Don and, by driving considerably faster than we cared for, he became British Motor Racing Champion and holder of the World Water Speed record.

Father kept a photographic record of our holidays, sticking the black-and-white prints neatly into albums, which I still have. So there we are, Mother and I, still enjoying the sunshine and fresh air, leaning on the railings on Brighton front, sitting in deckchairs on Eastbourne beach, walking in parks and over downland, Mother in her best hats and smartest clothes, I in the same short-trousered suit in which I went to school, and always wearing a tie: one did not buy special clothes for holidays, nor did one wear less than usual. There are photographs of the places we visited on excursions; Chichester Cross, Durley Dean, Alfriston, the Marlepins at Shoreham, Pevensey Castle (which was ivy-covered and derelict, and not at all the well-tended ruin it is today) and the paddle steamer, *Queen of the South*, in which we voyaged from Brighton to Worthing Pier and back, although Mother was a poor sailor and elected to return by bus. There are also snapshots of groups of long-forgotten guests at the private hotels in which we stayed.

There was the Hereward Hotel, at Cliftonville, where there were hosts of other children; the Cloncilla, in the square by the Wish Tower in Eastbourne; the Campo in Bognor; and in Brighton we stayed at the Palace Pier Hotel, which is still there, apparently unchanged, and later we went to the Hollywood, and then the Exeter. They were all comfortable and clean and respectable, and they served three good meals a day, including a four-course dinner with coffee in the lounge afterwards, and there was a set tea in the afternoon if you cared to go in for it, and if your capacity could stand it. We never paid more than three and a half guineas per week each, because it was not really necessary.

Most smaller hotels did not have constant hot water in the bedrooms, and a steaming metal jug was left outside the door at the time of the morning call. Service charges were not added to the bill, and at the end of the holiday there was always a discussion as to how much should be left on the dressing-table for the chambermaid. The waitress and the porter were dealt with in person.

We did not spend a great deal of time on the beach, because it was not until the mid-thirties that sunbathing became fashionable and, as a child, I was never very keen on swimming. Mother's great delight was to listen to the band, and we would sit in deckchairs by the bandstand for the morning concert. Each item was introduced by the bandmaster, who sometimes gave roguish glances at seemingly unattached ladies in the front rows, and who acknowledged applause by tearing off a dashing salute. I hated the whole ritual, especially the solo items by strangulated tenors and plump cornetists, and would bury myself in *The Boy's Magazine*.

Holidays were a festival of reading. Every day I bought a boy's paper, and kept an eye open for the bargain offers which were made by vendors on the beach: if you bought the current issue of *Answers* (2d) you received a free back number of *The Happy Mag* (7d) with a corner cut off to show that it had been remaindered.

If band concerts were boring, concert parties were another matter: I revelled in them and would attend two, or even three, performances in a day, if I could manage it. Brighton was especially rich in them, with one on the beach between the piers, and another on the beach towards Black Rock, and a third on the end of the Palace Pier. You were allowed to stand at the back for nothing, but were expected to put a penny or two in the box when a member of the company brought it round, rattling it under people's noses; and it was well worth the money to be so close to one of those god-like performers, so close indeed that you could see clearly the line where his brown make-up ended, halfway between his chin and the ruff of his pierrot costume. By the end of the fortnight, I knew many of the comedy items by heart.

On several evenings during our holidays, we would go to a theatre, and I can remember every play we saw. Sometimes it would be a prior-to-London tour, and then one would feel superior when it opened in the West End, and could say, airily, 'Oh, I saw that a long time ago.' On one occasion, at the Pier Theatre, Eastbourne, we went to the very first performance anywhere of a thriller called *The Lonely House*, and saw the authoress, Mrs Belloc Lowndes, take a bow – but unfortunately it was not a very good play. We saw *The Blue Peter* by E. Temple Thurston, and A. A. Milne's *Mr Pim Passes By*, and a very exciting play called *The Cat's Paw* by someone named Theophilus Charlton, and Frederick Lonsdale's *The Last of Mrs Cheyney*, with one of the best first-act curtains ever devised, and, at Brighton Hippodrome, an English version of a *Folies Bergères* revue. I think Father had some doubts about taking me to see that, but he need not have worried because my most vivid memory is of Robert Chisholm, with a blood-stained bandage round his head, singing 'Le Rêve Passe' – although, now I come to think of it, there were some very scantily clad ladies adorning a big golden crown in a finale depicting Napoleon's coronation.

There were other holiday spectacles, too: there was the lady diver who performed at the end of the West Pier, Brighton, every morning, and the slot machine which showed you a scale model of an execution for a penny, and there were splendid occupations like Skeeball and donkey rides. It was awful when you started saying to yourself that the day after the day after tomorrow we'd be going home, and then the day after tomorrow, and then tomorrow, and then you were off in a taxi to the station.

Also in the snapshot albums are pictures of a notable family event, the golden wedding of my mother's parents. There was a family party at the little house in Hampton Wick, and Mother made a huge cake decorated with golden sovereigns, which were no longer legal tender, of course, but they were easy to turn into cash.

I was fond of my grandparents' garden, because all we had at home was a wretched yard, in which the only greenery was a dusty loganberry bush which miraculously fruited every year. The Hampton Wick garden, although small, was countrified, and was a riot of lilies of the valley, forget-me-nots and London pride, with an enormous gooseberry bush which produced the biggest, squashiest pink gooseberries I have ever come across.

There were wonders in the house, too – that old grey parrot, for instance, and a huge pink shell in which I really could hear the sound of the sea, and lustres which tinkled, and a china ashtray in the shape of a monkey, and a mummified frog which had not survived an exceptionally dry summer; and some relics of Louisiana, such as the rattles from the tail of a rattlesnake, and some dried flowers from a bouquet presented to the wife of President McKinley.

There was no doubt that Grandfather was a hoarder, a failing which I have inherited from him. When his wife died, he was not well enough to run the little house on his own, so the sorrowing old man was put into furnished rooms in Kingston, where he could be looked after and where he pined away within a few months. Before disposing of the house, my mother had the sad task of sorting, and mostly destroying, his immense archive of press cuttings, theatre programmes, passenger lists, menus, letters and souvenirs.

Apart from the summer holidays, the only travelling was an occasional day trip to Maidstone with Father. My paternal grandfather had died soon after the turn of the century. A dedicated churchman, he was attending his friend, the Reverend Canon Samuel Joy, Vicar of Maidstone, and was at the Canon's bedside in the 14th-century vicarage when he himself was stricken and fell. Paralysed, he was carried the few yards to Knightrider House, where he died early the next morning.

Obviously, after Grandfather's death, a smaller dwelling was called for, and the house I used to visit was quite a modest one called Atholstone, in Buckland Road. My grandmother was not of a very advanced age – she was 66 when I was born – but she acted very old indeed. Wearing a braided black dress, ornamented with jet and relieved only by a white collar, she wore a white lace cap at all times; she was the Widow of Windsor all over again.

She was surrounded by a selection of daughters; there were always two or three in the house. She had had five, and only two had married, Grace to a surveyor in Rochester and Maud to a tea planter in Assam. Maud had killed herself only six weeks after her wedding in Calcutta Cathedral. Family gossip said it was because she had discovered the existence of a native mistress.

The unmarried daughters at Atholstone were, inevitably, nurses. Edith, the eldest, I remember as a stern-visaged woman; Eva, the one I liked, was comparatively jolly, and Mabel was a rather elusive creature who had a considerable reputation in the field of private nursing, and was often away caring for a member of one of the best families.

When it was fine, Eva would take me to play in the long, narrow garden, which was fascinating because it was laid out on a steep slope going down to a railway siding, and I could climb the wall and look down on lines of goods wagons, and across to the Sharp's Kreemy Toffee factory; or sometimes she would take me on an excursion to see Kit's Coty House, a cromlech near Aylesford, or, if the weather was poor, to the museum where the prime exhibit, so far as I was concerned, was a macabre little set-piece in a glass case, with two stuffed kittens mischievously ransacking a lady's work-basket, unravelling balls of wool and playing with cotton reels.

On the whole, I did not look forward to the Maidstone excursions because there was an atmosphere of formality and faded gentility, and I remembered a luncheon when my hearty attacks on a plate of cold mutton caused two forks in succession of the worn family silver to buckle in my hand.

2

My first school, at the age of five, was Park Lodge, a girls'
school with kindergarten attached, in the centre of the town.
At morning assembly, the infants were put among the girls,
who seemed to me to be large and rather noisy. I cannot
remember learning anything at the school, but I do remember
experiencing the first *frissons* of sex. Once a week, we went
across the road to a YMCA hall for physical exercises. The
kindergarten class was followed by a class of girls, all of whom
removed their frocks as they came into the hall, and I found
their rounded forms in vests and knickers most interesting.

At the end of term, there was a concert, in which I made
my first appearance on any stage. The infants were formed into
a make-believe band, marching round the stage pretending to
play toy instruments, and I was given a trumpet. The boy
behind me trod on one of my heels, taking my plimsoll off the
back of my foot, so that I was hopping round on the other foot
trying to pull it back into place, which was difficult while
pretending to play the trumpet. It was an inauspicious debut.

I was at Park Lodge only two terms because nits were discovered in my hair, which horrified my parents. Instead they
sent me to Elmhurst, a private school for boys only. Looking
back, I suppose it was not all that bad, and there was one
master, Stanley Goddard, who was imaginative and interesting,
but there seemed an almost total lack of supervision outside

the classroom, and there were no games except some singularly rough ones organized by the boys themselves.

One day I was fetched by my father to be taken home to lunch, and we walked down Penrhyn Road with Sergeant Bryant, a tall ex-army drill instructor with a spiky moustache, who did some part-time work at the school. In response to Father's questioning, Bryant confirmed his suspicions that the school left a fair amount to be desired, and added that in his opinion the best local school was Gate House, to which he also contributed his services: at that school, said the sergeant, there was 'the team spirit', an inspiring phrase which was echoed several times by both men.

So I went to Gate House, where I stayed for six years. There is no doubt at all that it was a very good preparatory school indeed, and it became better as it became bigger. When I first went there, it was in modest premises opposite Norbiton Church, but later it moved to the top of Kingston Hill where it occupied a large house called Cumberland Lodge and, soon afterwards, absorbed a neighbouring school with spacious grounds, called The Grange. The proprietor and headmaster was a small, grey-haired, rather frightening man named H. D. Moseley, who was known as Old Man. Nobody was allowed to slack and, in Latin and mathematics particularly, the standard was very high. I have no doubt that there was plenty of 'team spirit', but it was never allowed to be obtrusive.

Every day, we finished lessons at four-thirty, then stayed at school for tea, a metallic beverage from an urn. We were supplied with three pieces of bread and butter and one piece of bread and jam — if you wanted cake, you brought it yourself. Then we did our preparation, under supervision, until seven o'clock. It made a long day.

My parents thought it would be good for me to walk for two of the four daily journeys, so each morning I collected two-pence, for two penny fares. Naturally, I spent this on a boys' paper on my way to school, which meant that I had to walk all four times, whatever the weather. There was a curious but strong parental prejudice against buses, and I was allowed to take only trams, which travelled the same route. I gathered that this was a safety precaution, but as I had to venture out into the middle of the road to board a tram, whereas a bus drove right in to the kerb, I could never see where the extra safety came in. In fact, a boy named Squire fell off the top of a tram one day, and hurt himself quite badly, but nobody ever fell off the top of a bus.

One afternoon, when I was ten, Old Man organized an excursion to Wimbledon Theatre to see Sir Frank Benson's Company play Shakespeare's *Julius Caesar*. Afterwards, he took us all out to tea, but I was in too much of a daze to appreciate it. A new world had been opened to me, and I was hearing over and over in my head the voice of Benson, who had played Anthony, speaking the line, 'This was the noblest Roman of them all'. Could other Shakespeare plays be as wonderful as that, if transferred from cold print and the schoolroom to the stage? But there were no more theatre excursions. The next Shakespeare play I saw was several years later, when my mother took me to see some Stock Exchange amateurs play *The Merchant of Venice*, again at Wimbledon Theatre – but the company generated no magic, and I remember the production as drab.

I had at last found a friend in the immediate neighbourhood. A lease on the adjoining 49 Fife Road was taken by a widow, Mrs Stark, who opened a sweet shop – and, in the view of a ten-year old, there can be few better local amenities. Her son, Ron, was a year or two older than I, but we found we shared many interests, such as back numbers of *The Nelson Lee Library* and fishing for newts in the pond on Ham Common. We seldom bothered to visit each other's houses but talked while hanging out of our adjoining top back bedroom windows, although occasionally we placed step ladders against the yard fence and climbed over.

During the summer, the Stark family sold ice-cream. It was a delicious, fresh, nourishing concoction, of a kind hard to find nowadays, because legislation demands that ice-cream may be manufactured only in a room devoted entirely to that purpose and, rather than go to such trouble and expense, the modern sweet shop proprietor has his ice-cream – and the second word is a mockery – delivered from some far-off factory, where it has been made from whale oil and gelatin, topped up with artificial flavouring and artificial colouring. Mrs Stark's ice-cream was made of milk, eggs and sugar, with a dash of vanilla essence, and it was usually made in the yard. The mixture was put into a tin, which was then enclosed in a wooden barrel full of ice and freezing salt; then a handle was turned, revolving the tin until its contents had solidified. I was happy to turn that handle for as long as required, in exchange for two wafer biscuits enclosing a thick wodge of the excellent mixture.

When Guy Fawkes Day came along, Ron was given more freedom than I in selecting fireworks. In view of my junior status, I was restricted to buying innocuous catherine wheels and golden rain and jumpers, while he was splashing out money on such sophisticated items as thunder flashes, devils-among-the-tailors and whistling rockets. I was at my favourite vantage point, leaning out of my bedroom window to get a good aerial view, when he gave his display to an audience of me, his mother and his sister, Betty. There came a moment when the entire district was rent by cascades, cannonades, flashes, smoke and major explosions. 'What's that one called, Ron?' I called out, in admiration. There was no reply, as the entire Stark family had run for cover, because a spark had ignited the whole expensive boxful at once.

Our friendship came to an end when my parents overheard Ron and me telling each other some rather doubtful stories. It was thought that perhaps the companionship of the older boy was bad for me. It was no use arguing, of course; although Ron freely admitted that I was better at telling the stories than he was.

One of my best friends at Gate House was Dicky Jones, who lived with his mother, a younger sister and two older brothers in a large house with a big, wild garden, in Hampton Wick. Having been brought up in a disciplined and conventional way, I was fascinated by the family's way of life. Perhaps the fact that they had lived in India had something to do with it, but if I called at half past ten in the morning, I was likely to find the whole family still in bed because nobody had felt like getting up. There was a similar elasticity in meal times, although at any hour of the day we were likely to be summoned by Mrs Jones to deal with a pile of delicious hot chupatis. Dangerous battles were fought in the garden shrubbery with airguns, but these came to an end when one warrior had to have a pellet extracted from his face perilously close to an eye.

One day, there was a royal occasion in Hampton Wick when Princess Mary, the Princess Royal, came to open a playing field in Bushey Park. I climbed one of the park walls to see her go by and, looking at it today, it must have been a daunting height for a small boy to scramble up, but perhaps patriotic fervour lent me strength. I followed the Princess about all the afternoon, and bought a glossy picture postcard of her in the uniform of the Girl Guides as a souvenir.

It was at about that time that I began to develop compulsive symptoms. On my way to school, I would feel impelled to place my feet on certain paving stones and not on others, and to touch certain objects a certain number of times. It was a form of propitiation, and I felt that if I did not do so, then something frightful would happen. The magical number was four – and it still is, come to that – and the objects had to be touched or kicked or stepped-on in multiples of that number, and preferably by both hands or both feet.

Psychologists say that it is no more than the overspill from an active brain, and that it is a harmless trait – after all, Dr Johnson had it – but in my case it was accompanied by more disturbing troubles. Worst of all was an anxiety that I might not be able to control my bodily functions: when I was invited by a neighbour to join his family on a motoring trip, I agonized for hours before leaving the house – suppose I felt my stomach failing me, what could I say? – where could I go? On a wet afternoon in Brighton, when Father offered to take me to a cinema to see a western, I told him shamefacedly of my fears that I might not be able to sit through the performance

45

— and wouldn't it be better if I stayed in the hotel? He nodded, understandingly, but wisely insisted that I went with him. Fortunately, it was a state of mind which did not last long.

Because I had become a dedicated radio listener, I would buy *Radio Times* each week on my way home from school. One of my early memories, as a toddler, is of my Uncle Percy leading me to a big black contraption which he had built in a corner of his dining-room, and putting a pair of earphones on my head. 'Listen,' he said, 'you'll hear a man talking, a long way away.' Indeed, it seemed a very long way away that a faint, tinny voice was saying incomprehensible things, in what was probably signals jargon. I was not impressed.

My next experience was when I went with Mother to see a builder named Mr Chambers, who was doing some repairs to the house. Like Uncle Percy, he was a radio buff, and was the owner of a big, black contraption. While he and my mother discussed business, he gave me a pair of headphones. With no enthusiasm, I put them to my ears, and heard a jolly voice singing 'London Bridge is falling down'. These headphones made much more sense than Uncle Percy's, and I took an approving view.

Whether it was due to the influence of Mr Chambers, I do not know, but we acquired a radio receiver at home. It was a primitive one, consisting of a drum with wire wound round it, a small brass pot containing a crystal, and a piece of thin wire with which one poked the crystal until a sensitive spot was found. I suppose it was not strong enough to power a whole pair of headphones, because we had only a single earpiece which was put to one ear while a finger was stuffed in the other to keep out extraneous sounds. There was not very much to listen to, and the presentation of programmes was casual: quite frequently, the announcer would say, 'Please stand by for two minutes', which meant presumably that he was going to move the piano or go outside for a smoke.

Anyway, we were sufficiently impressed to buy a bigger set — a valve set which was strong enough to power three pairs of headphones, which were hung on hooks on the dining-room wall. Each pair had a long piece of flex, so that we were not too confined.

The first items I looked for in *Radio Times* were the programmes for 'Children's Hour', which was run as a part-time occupation by the announcers, who called themselves aunts and uncles for the occasion. There was Uncle Rex, and Uncle Jeff, who was the funny uncle, and Aunt Sophie, who played the piano, and Uncle Caractacus – now, there was a curious name for an uncle!

In the evenings, the concerts – they were not yet called programmes – consisted of a small orchestra, a couple of singers and a comedian. Most of the solo performers were modest after-dinner entertainers who were glad to earn an extra guinea or two in this strange new medium – and, as a result of their radio exposure, some of them became celebrated. Among the comedians were John Henry, a Yorkshireman who played funny sketches with his wife, Blossom, and his friend, Joe Murgatroyd; and Willie Rouse, known as Wireless Willie; and a blind entertainer at the piano named Ronald Gourley, and Helena Millais, a comedienne. A star attraction was a soft-voiced civil servant, who called himself A. J. Alan and told intriguing and amusing stories, always in the first person. Then there were the early broadcast plays which, to take advantage of the new blind medium, were often set in dark places, such as a coal mine or a lonely place at night.

One of the hazards for the listener was that the battery would run down in the middle of a play, so we had two, one in use and one spare. The depleted one was carried down to the electric light works, in a wire frame, to be recharged.

There were two events which gave great impetus to broadcasting: the first was the opening of the 1924 British Empire Exhibition at Wembley by King George V. It was an historic occasion; for the first time the voice of a king was to be heard in the homes of his subjects. My grandparents, who were radioless, came over from Hampton Wick to listen on our set, and my parents' pairs of headphones were divided, so that four people could listen: although I was allowed to retain my full pair. Strangely enough, it did not occur to anyone at the BBC to record this unique event, and many years later they broadcast an appeal: had any listener recorded the King's voice? Several had and now a recording is safely preserved in the archives.

The second event was the General Strike of 1926. There were no newspapers, other than token single sheets and the four-page *The British Gazette*, edited by Winston Churchill, and rumours were rife. For the duration of the strike, copyright in BBC news bulletins, which was held by Reuter, Press Association, Exchange Telegraph and Central News, was lifted, and listeners were invited to pass on the broadcast news by any means available to them. Conscientious citizens made transcripts of the main items from the bulletins and displayed them outside their houses.

At school, I took a pioneer role in a craze, which raged during two successive winters, for publishing unofficial magazines, and a few copies have survived. The first issue of *The Gate House and Grange Gazette* consisted of eight pages and was handwritten; the price on the masthead was one penny, but the labour of writing out complete copies was obviously too great, so I charged a halfpenny for a read. On the front page were some 'Side Splitters', obviously culled from column-fillers in popular weeklies; Page 2 consisted of 'Our Notice Board' and an editorial; then came four pages of a school story called *Dooley's Dictaphone*, cribbed, if I remember right, from *Chums*; page 7 was devoted to 'Our Competition', which invited readers to make a list of the films of the cowboy star Tom Mix, the sender of the longest list to receive an unspecified prize; and on the back page were some quite pungent reviews of fiction available in the school library. *'The Warlord of Mars*, a wierd [sic] story of adventure on the planet Mars. Thrilling but difficult to understand. *Rollingson and I*. Very well written, but rather dull.'

The following winter I was publisher, editor and author of *The School Gazette*, of which four issues survive. The first was again handwritten, but consisted of only four pages, and sold at a halfpenny. There were more jokes, some school news, the Tom Mix competition (I had already learned the golden rule about making a little go a long way) and some new book reviews, although *The Warlord of Mars* came in for further attention. ('Highly improbable, but good reading.')

For the following three issues, technology took over, and they were printed, inadequately, on a jelly press. I had co-opted a co-editor named Lilley, but the editorial policy remained the same. No. 2 contained a two-page story, *Sir Richard's Run*, by F. R. Plomley, which is about Dick Turpin (I think, but the printing is very indistinct indeed). No. 3 was a Specially Enlarged Edition of twelve pages. It contained a second instalment of *Sir Richard's Run*, which reveals itself as a two-part serial (and indeed about Dick Turpin) and a four-page story, *The Red Triangle*, featuring Jim Conway, the detective, and his assistant, Fred, by a boy named Dimott. Obviously, the circulation was reasonably satisfactory, since contributions were invited at a payment of 2d per page. For No. 3, Dymott (the spelling had changed) wrote another adventure of Jim Conway and Fred, and this time it ran to four-and-a-half pages – I hope he received his 9d, which was a lot of money in our circle – and I contributed the first instalment of a comedy serial called *The Tin-Lizzie*, of which the remaining instalments, if they ever existed, are irretrievably lost.

I have also found a copy of a rival publication, *The School Mail*, edited and published 'entirely by the boarders', which was a lie for a start, because four of the ten jellypressed pages are in the handwriting of one of the masters. Its contents list closely follows that of its senior competitor, *The School Gazette*.

The magazine business escalated, and three or four publications were on sale in the school grounds at the same time. Competition was so keen that violence was not unknown, and I have seen an editor in tears when thugs in the employ of a rival concern had dumped the entire 'run' of a new issue in a muddy puddle.

At the age of thirteen, I was despatched by my mother to

49

take lessons in ballroom dancing. I did not protest, because it seemed quite a sophisticated thing to do. Mrs Grove, a friend of hers, had a daughter named Molly who had just passed her examinations, and a studio had been built for her across the width of the garden of their house in Staunton Road. The studio was not very large, but it was large enough. It smelt of new wood and French chalk, which was scattered on the floor to make it slippery, and it was quite bare, except for a wind-up gramophone on a table in a corner, and a row of second-hand theatre seats bolted to a wall.

Molly was a pretty, dark girl with large eyes and unruly hair. (As Molly Glessing, she was to do quite well playing character roles in Hollywood.) Each week I would go for a private lesson, and I quite enjoyed taking this attractive young lady respectfully in my arms and allowing her to instruct me in the foxtrot, the waltz, the tango and, as a fun finale, the charleston.

She gave practice dances in the studio from time to time and, with a bit of a squeeze, there was room for eight or nine couples. Those who attended were mainly Mother and her friends, and there was a grave shortage of men; however, I did my bit and solemnly guided a variety of middle-aged partners round the confined space. During my adult years, I have never been much of a man for the dancefloor, but it has been useful to know the rules, and on at least one occasion I have been paid money for dancing in public.

My later years at Gate House were marred by bullying. There was a boy who was a born bully: he was not taller than me, but stronger and more powerfully built and, for some reason, he picked on me as his victim. He was half German and had blond cropped hair in the Teutonic manner: when he made his sadistic advances, he looked like a leering, toothy frog. One day in the gym, the instructor – Sergeant Bryant had been succeeded by the younger and spryer Petty-Officer Skinner – matched the two of us with boxing-gloves on. I anticipated a hiding as the blond beast squared up to me, but I broke through his guard and knocked him to the floor. I looked down at him and, to my amazement, he was blubbing. I called out to Petty-Officer Skinner, 'Sir, I think he's hurt.' Soft-hearted idiot that I was: I often feel regret that I was not quick-witted enough to hit him again on his way down!

Unless one wished, because of family associations, to move on to one of the senior public schools, Mr Moseley recommended to parents that they should consider King's College School which, after a start in the basement of King's College in the Strand, was now at Wimbledon, only five or six miles away, and catering mainly for day boys. I knew that a few years for me at King's would make a considerable dent in the Plomley finances, especially as Father had recently had a stroke which, although fortunately a mild one, had left him with restricted use of his right arm. Nevertheless, he gallantly decided that priority should be given to my education, and I set to work to pass my Common Entrance examination.

My one memory of that long-ago scholastic event is my discovery that it is a sound rule, when dealing with any problem, to try to project oneself into the mind of any other person concerned. We had been given access to a set of the previous year's papers, to show us what we were up against, and one of the English history questions was: 'What were the dates of accession of all the kings named Edward to sit on the throne of England since the Norman Conquest?' A good question, I thought to myself, and if I were setting the current year's questions I would save myself trouble by asking for the dates of all the Henrys – and my guess was right. My English history marks, at any rate, were not bad.

Having been accepted for King's, Father and I went to be interviewed by my future headmaster, H. Lionel Rogers, MA, a lean, aquiline man with a heavy moustache. 'I am a poor man, Mr Rogers,' said my father, 'and if there is any scholarship he can enter for . . .' A scholarship! Me? I had a very low opinion of my scholastic abilities.

To leave a prep school, where one has enjoyed senior status, to become part of the small fry in a junior form at a public school is a traumatic experience. On my first day it seemed as if there were thousands of boys surging about the buildings, some with grown-up voices and at least one with a moustache. I was carried with the throng, clattering up stone steps into the vast, shadowy Great Hall, with tapestries of St George and St Michael, and portraits on the panelled walls of distinguished Old Boys and previous headmasters. Mr Rogers, in mortarboard and gown, stood at a lectern on the platform and made announcements about school matters which were incomprehensible to me; then there was a great deal of reading out of lists of names, and eventually I found myself, with twenty others, in the classroom of Lower IVA. I was to be in the top Latin set, which was a tribute to Old Man's teaching, but in the bottom set for French, which was not surprising, because we had had only two hours of French a week compared with seven and a half hours of Latin.

The notice boards were covered with announcements of Rugby fixtures, OTC events and the Hobbies Competition while, left over from the summer term, were yellowing lists of cricket and cross-country teams. There were also posters publicizing the Literary Society, the Natural History Society, the Museum, the Union, the Christian Union, the Radio Society, the Botanical Gardens and the Engineering Society. Obviously being at King's was a full-time job. I was approached by the secretary of the Botanical Gardens, which consisted of a small patch divided into even smaller patches, and invited to join. I knew nothing about gardening and even less about botany, but I was flattered at being asked, and I said yes. It appeared that the group had fallen on hard times, and the membership was small and unenthusiastic. I spent a few lunch hours tending a patch of perennials, but most of my time was devoted to squirting water about and eventually I was asked to leave.

During my first terms at King's, I was an abject failure. My idea of what life at a public school should be was based on the hundreds of school stories I had read, and I ragged about far too much, and gave a performance of a cheeky fourth-former which was appreciated by nobody: I was unruly, untidy and slack. I worked well only during the English periods of E. R.

Thompson, a relaxed ex-soldier who really loved books and had missionary zeal to make boys read them. In me, he found ready collaboration, and he began to guide my tastes most skilfully. He spent the minimum time on grammar and analysis, and spurred us on to use our imaginations in such ingenious exercises as writing new endings to H. G. Wells short stories.

I was not to work with Eric Whelpton, the other master who made a lasting impression on me, until later. Eric, who became, and still is, a friend, has a commanding presence and a superb gift of the gab. He inspired our interest in modern languages, of which he is equally at home in four, by informed and fascinating talk about their practical use. Very sensibly, he left scholastic life to write travel books and two outstanding volumes of autobiography, *The Making of a European* and *The Making of an Englishman*.

On Monday afternoons, we paraded in uniform as members of the Officers Training Corps. I enjoyed the military life, although I was not smart enough to reach non-commissioned rank, and it appealed to my sense of drama and make-believe to crawl through undergrowth, firing blank cartridges. On one occasion I played a splendid court martial scene. A friend named Dennis Peters had been pounced on by a zealous sergeant for appearing on parade with inadequately cleaned webbing equipment, and he had been ordered to stay after parade to clean it. I told him not to bother to do so because I would lend him mine, which I did, and he took it to the sergeant, who approved it. Foolishly, I boasted of the success of the ruse. Some false friend informed on us, and Dennis and I were marched to the Company Office with all the trimmings of shouted commands of 'Prisoners and escort, ten-shun'. I was the first to be questioned by the Duty Officer, who asked, 'Do you plead Guilty or Not Guilty?' I threw back my head, thrust out my chin and looked him steadily in the eyes with a steadfast gaze. 'Guilty, sir,' I replied, in a ringing tone that was confident and unashamed. 'Have you anything to say in extenuation?' he asked. With an even more true-blue glint in my eyes, I cried, dramatically, 'Nothing, sir.' Even Dennis, to whom I had been displaying my clean-cut profile, told me it was a good performance, as we wearily ran round the cricket field, undergoing the punishment drill to which we had been sentenced.

PD is a very sensible form of punishment; it is boring, but it does one good, and it does not ruin handwriting, as does the senseless scribbling of lines. If you were given more than three PDs in a term, or two in a week, you were handed a report card, which was a way of putting you on your very best behaviour. At the beginning of every lesson, for a week, you were required to put the card on the master's desk, and collect it at the end with his initialled comment, 'S' (satisfactory) or 'NS' (non-satisfactory). If you collected three NSs you also collected a headmaster's beating, which was a rare distinction.

On one occasion, I was put directly on report without a preliminary PD by a languages master named Duval, better known to us as 'Bogey'. I considered this unjust, and I had the infernal cheek to ask to see the headmaster to complain about the matter. Looking back, I am amazed at, and grateful for, the tolerance shown by Mr Rogers, who listened patiently, explained that my first and only duty was to do as I was told, and sent me on my way.

At the end of my first year, I made another stage appearance. A friend of my mother's was a music teacher named Stella Sawyer who, despite a gentle and simpering manner, had considerable and persistent enterprise. She had come unstuck in an attempt to launch trademark collecting as a hobby, finding herself unable to dispose of a large number of albums she had ordered to be printed and bound before discovering that nobody wanted to collect trademarks – which shows that market research must have its uses. She then wrote an operetta, *The Minstrel Queen*, which she decided to put on herself.

She scratched around among her pupils, friends and acquaintances to get a cast together, and must indeed have reached the bottom of the barrel when she invited me along for a voice test. I was only fourteen, but my voice had broken early, and I suppose I must have possessed some slight curiosity value as a small boy with a deep, booming voice. Probably to her surprise, and certainly to mine, I found I could reproduce with reasonable accuracy the notes she struck on the piano, because I knew nothing about music and, as the phrase so tellingly has it, did not know a B flat from a bull's foot. Anyway, she needed a bass who could go down to a G above bottom G, and I was one, even if undersized, so I was given the part. In fact, as the casting situation got more and more desperate, I ended up with three parts.

Eventually, Miss Sawyer managed to enlist the entire dramatic section of the local branch of the Junior Imperial League, and we began rehearsals. The word operetta evokes a mental picture of lively goings-on among *midinettes* or Greek goddesses, but this was a rather solemn piece about warfare between the Spaniards and the Moors, with a predictably pro-Spanish bias. It began with a scene of rejoicing in the Spanish court, with the Queen and all her courtiers singing 'Joy, Joy, Joy, the day of war is ended', and then Don Alonso – that was me, with a moustache and a small beard – rushed on and put an end to the festivities with,

What means all this rejoicing?
Why all this senseless mirth?
– Your King a captive – your country vanquished –
Why all this mock'ry – ?

and on the last syllable I dropped an octave to that G, and then finished with an impassioned 'Tell me why'. I then reported, in more detail and in spoken dialogue which had been written out for me on a page from a trademark album, to the Queen, played by a blond girl called Pinky, who announced that she was going to disguise herself as a minstrel and cross into the Moorish lines to liberate her lord and master. It was stirring stuff, marred so far as I was concerned by the fact that the costumiers had sent me a sword with a broken scabbard, so that the end flapped about ridiculously and I could not get my sword back into it after I had flourished it.

My second appearance was on the opposing side, as one of the henchmen of Abu Ben Hafid, the Moorish chieftain, and then I turned up for the third time as the jailer who admitted the Minstrel Queen into the cell where her husband was incarcerated, which was the obvious point for the principal love duet.

We gave one performance at the Surbiton Assembly Rooms, to recoup some of the production expenses, and another in a church hall in aid of an organ fund. I admired the way the indomitable composer/librettist/producer/conductor adjusted herself to circumstances. She managed to get together a complete cast, with a sizable chorus as well, but she had to take what she could get so far as the orchestra was concerned, and I can imagine her rescoring madly as instrumentalists either promised their services or quit. According to the programme, the orchestra finally consisted of four first violins, three second violins, one cello, one flute, two triangles, a tambourine, castenets, drums and piano.

The experience had a considerable effect on me. The colour, the lights, the music, the excitement of performing – and probably the proximity of all the girls taking part – pushed me further towards being stagestruck.

The show must have been a success, because it was revived a few months later but, to my chagrin, I was not allowed to take part, because Father had been to see my form master, and had been appalled at the report he was given. Neither was I allowed to take part in Miss Sawyer's next brainchild, which was about Cavaliers and Roundheads, and which was given its world première in Hampton Wick.

The thing that pulled me up by my bootstraps at King's was my decision to shoot instead of playing cricket, which I had always considered a boring game. As my record on the miniature range was good I was accepted for the Bisley party, a select group which spent two afternoons a week on the ranges and which could hardly have been considered to be overworked. After a sandwich lunch in the motor coach on the way down, we each fired a sighter and seven shots at the 200 yards range, and then the same at 500 yards, after which we had a enormous tea in the clubhouse of the Surrey Rifle Association, followed by ginger beer shandy. To those who protested that we had an easy option, we would point out that we had to clean our rifles as well.

The fact that I have a slow heartbeat may have something to do with it, but I was a fair shot. During my first shooting summer, I was selected as one of the Cadet Pair to shoot for the school during Bisley Fortnight, which meant that, having represented King's against all comers, I was entitled to wear a colours tie, and the only others who could do so, apart from my fellow Cadet, were members of the first cricket XI, the first Rugby XV and the shooting VIII, all of whom were considerably older. This gave me some confidence and a minor sense of achievement, which was exactly what I needed to sort me out. The following year, I was in the VIII and shot for the Ashburton Shield, as well as winning a medal in the Sussex Public Schools Competition. However, these small triumphs went for nothing when I failed to pass my School Certificate.

Father had been hoping against hope that I would do well in the examination, because I would have been granted Matriculation exemption, and he had a theory that Matric was very important, proving to any prospective employer that one had received a reasonable education up to university standard. As family finances were now at a very low ebb, and as there was no guarantee that I would succeed if I stayed at King's for another year, he told me that he was going to take me away and send me to a crammer for intensive coaching.

Before departing for ten days of OTC camp at Tidworth Pennings, I was given a farewell interview by the headmaster: it was the first time we had spoken since I had called on him to complain. He asked me what I was going to do. I replied that I was going to be tutored. He nodded, and asked me what I was going to do after that. I said that I didn't know, but there had been talk of my going to a business school. He did not actually wince, but I think he looked pained. He stood up to give me a farewell handshake.

I felt that some little speech was called for from me, so I stammered out, 'Goodbye, sir. I've enjoyed myself very much at King's.' He probably gathered what I meant, but we both knew that I had not expressed myself very well.

There was a little choking feeling in my throat as I walked away towards the railway station. It was true that I had enjoyed myself, even if I did not leave trailing clouds of glory.

Some weeks before the end of term, in a kindly gesture to celebrate my one small distinction, Father had told me that he would have the shooting badges from the sleeve of my tunic mounted in a frame, together with the medal I had won, and alongside them he would put the summer's fixture list giving the scores of our weekly matches. He asked me to go to the school notice board and copy down the figures: he asked me day after day, but I still forgot to do so. I have the framed souvenir still – and there are blank spaces where the scores should be. It serves me right.

One thing the school lacked was musical life. On Speech Day, there was a concert, at which a few masters and some Old Boys contributed ballads, and songs from the Gilbert and Sullivan operas, and a scratch orchestra, assembled from heaven knew where, cautiously picked its way through the *Rosamunde* Overture, but I do not remember any other concert, nor was I ever invited to attend a record recital: there was not even a dance band. I joined the choir, because *The Minstrel Queen* had shown me that I liked to try to sing, and because I enjoyed sprawling in the shadows with the other basses at after-school practices in the Great Hall – even if I was occasionally reprimanded for grunting away an octave too low. I think I might have responded to music if anyone had taken me in hand, but I had no confidence in my ability in the subject, and I still have not.

There was no drama at King's either. Once I tried to organize a production of J. J. Bell's one-act play, *Thread o'Scarlet*, which I had seen the Kingston Imps present, but there was nobody to whom I could turn for help.

Every year, there was the Hobbies competition. It was an

58

interhouse affair, and therefore everyone had to take part. All the exhibits were laid out in one of the science laboratories, and the judges went round and awarded points. Those who, like myself, dabbled in a number of interests but had no serious hobby were reduced to baking cakes or making toffee: there were hundredweights of toffee laid out on the benches, most of it obviously inedible. Fortunate was the boy who could hurriedly reassemble his father's stamp or coin collection. One year, I joined the toffee-makers, and another year I wrote a short story about aerial warfare. It was announced that the headmaster would judge the literary entries, but I surmise that he was not impressed with my story, because I received no comment, nor was my manuscript returned. I cannot remember what I submitted during my third year.

It was possibly because of a lack of interest in the arts that homosexuality was not overt in the school. At the time I was completely ignorant that it existed, but when I look back I can pinpoint no group of probable participants. The repertoire of not-very-funny dirty stories which circulated was completely heterosexual, there were many furtive references to masturbation and there was, of course, a healthy curiosity about the female body. One 14-year-old claimed to have been seduced by the family maid, and he was frequently quizzed about his enviable experience.

On returning from camp, I went to Norfolk to stay for a week or two at Holly House, in the delightfully named hamlet of Dumpling Green, near East Dereham. Some cousins of Mother's lived there, drawing ice-cold water from a well, using a double-seater privy, and bravely walking up and down a back staircase which had once been boarded up because of the persistent nocturnal appearances of a done-wrong-by lady who had drowned herself in the pond in the adjoining meadow centuries before. Among the other attractions was a lovely old barn in which, if you stood in a certain spot, you could produce a quite sensational sequence of echoes. There was no electricity or gas, and one went to bed by candlelight.

I was particularly drawn to Great-Uncle Jermyn, a frail,

scholarly old gentleman who had more or less retired to the eighteenth century. He spent his days enjoying his battered old calf-bound books, and he delighted in showing me the collection of engravings and caricatures which covered his walls, chuckling with glee as he pointed out some particularly telling piece of malicious absurdity.

I had stayed in the house before, and had got to know many of the young people who lived nearby, and the days passed swiftly, with cycle rides about the flat countryside, games of tennis on parched grass courts and swimming in the River Wensum, all the memories of which are flooded with the hot sunshine which seems a constant part of youth.

When I went home, I was presented to Mr J. P. Long, BA, who was to take over my instruction. He was fat, deaf, elderly and a first-rate teacher. He held his daily classes in the vestry of St Mary's, a beautiful little Georgian church near Teddington Lock, which had been superceded by St Alban's, a huge copper-roofed establishment across the road. I did not know it then, but one of the graves in the disused churchyard was that of one of my great-grandfathers, Charles Henderson, tailor, of Teddington.

There were eight or nine of us who sat round the long green-baize-covered table, working for various examinations. There was Roger Pertwee, late of Taunton School and resigned to taking up banking, with whom I struck up an immediate friendship (he was to be killed in the war); two ex-Radleyan brothers named Orde; a cheerful, bespectacled young man named Oliver Higgs; a young Cockney, whose name I forget, who was given to outrageous innuendo; a student of theology named Frank Collard-Scruby; a daunting young woman named Miss Fair, with whom the rest of us never got on Christian name terms, who was studying to become a missionary, and Peggy Mould, who was dark, willowy and very pretty. She and I used sometimes to stay in the vestry during the lunch hour and cook sausages on a gas-fire which made popping noises when kicked. On several occasions she permitted me to take her to the cinema, and she once allowed me to kiss her when we happened to be sitting side-by-side on the vestry table but, alas, she did not otherwise encourage my attentions.

Mr Long's deafness enabled us to get away with a certain amount of fooling, and when one of the Ordes, who was a fair musician, was thundering out jazz on the church organ, Long's only comment was a muttered imprecation about the nuisance of street musicians. He was the only man I have ever met to indulge in the habit of chewing cloves all day.

At mid-morning, one of the boys would remember that he had forgotten to post a letter, and that would remind others of telephone calls which must be made, and most of the males would go across to the Anglers to drink beer or shandy. If we were away too long, Miss Fair would be sent to fetch us back, which she was delighted to do because she was a worker in the cause of total abstinence.

I still had no idea what I wanted to do — or rather I did have an idea but it seemed too far-fetched to be worth mentioning: I wanted to work in the theatre, or one of the ancillary forms of theatre, such as films or broadcasting — I wanted to perform and I wanted to write. To start with I would settle for the most humble form of employment in that magic world.

Where this obsession came from, I have often wondered. Of course, the excitement of visits to Kingston Empire, seeing Sir Frank Benson's company play *Julius Caesar* at Wimbledon Theatre, and the countless hours I had spent in cinemas must have contributed, and so had my appearance in *The Minstrel Queen*, and there is no doubt that my encounters with Billy Watts did too. One of my mother's best friends was Mrs Watts, a stylish widow with two sons. The younger, Guy, was a playmate of mine, and his brother, Billy, who was considerably older, was an actor. He was not a very successful actor and never worked in the theatre, as he had a position in a family business which made touring impossible, but he played frequently in films. He was a good-looking young man, and had somehow become typecast as a reporter: he was to be seen in picture after picture, with his hat on the back of his head, interviewing the hero or the heroine and scribbling rapidly in a notebook. To think that Billy actually mixed with all those glamorous people I saw on the screen . . . in fact, he was one of them. I regarded him with awe.

Once, Guy took me into Billy's bedroom to see his picture gallery. Every young man should have a hobby, and Billy's was girls: on the walls were dozens of glossy photographs of actresses, some of them wearing very little, and there were piles of magazines featuring similar camera studies. On one occasion when I visited the house Billy had another actor as a guest, a large man named Tubby Phillips, who actually featured in a set of cigarette cards of British film players, and there was usually a girl friend there too – and invariably a pretty one. The more I came into contact with show business, the more I liked it. On my frequent visits to the reading room at the public library I used to study *The Stage* to see what was going on.

My father, long resigned to the fact that I wanted no part of the medical world, had given me a book, *On Leaving School*, written by a captain of industry, in the hope that it would spark off an idea or an ambition. Dutifully, I thumbed through it, but it was all about industry and sales management and average adjusting, with not a single word about the performing arts, so I did not read it.

One day, when I returned from Teddington, Father told me that he had seen in the *Surrey Comet* that a local estate agency was advertising for a young man to learn the business, and he suggested that I should apply. The agency, which had recently opened, was only about a hundred and fifty yards from home, so nothing could have been more convenient, and they seemed quite pleased to have me. Admittedly, the payment offered was only half-a-crown a week, but commission, they said, should bring this up to fifteen shillings, or even a pound; and the management would be prepared to let me work only during the afternoons until my examination was over. I knew nothing about estateagenting, but assumed that people would always want to live under cover, so I joined.

My schooldays were over: I was now a wage-earner — if half-a-crown a week could be considered a wage.

3

The offices of Marlows, Estate Agents, Surveyors and Valuers, consisted of half a shop, the other half being occupied by a coal order office, where two clerks sat at a long, high desk. The firm was run by a smooth, fair-haired man named Nunn, with an assistant named Eagle. The advertisement had produced three replies, and all three applicants had been snapped up – at half-a-crown a week.

There was a branch office on the Kingston bypass, consisting of a hut on the grass verge. A big new estate of cheap semi-detached houses was being built, and Marlows had been appointed agents for their sale. Most of my afternoons would be spent at the branch office, where there was little going on and where I would have plenty of opportunity to study. I could sit either in the hut or in a show house, which had been furnished by Messrs Arding and Hobbs, and where there was a coal fire. As none of the windows or doors in the show house fitted, there were hellish draughts, so I preferred the hut and its smelly oil stove. Nobody ever came to buy a house: in fact, the only potential purchasers who came my way were two men in a car who drove up and said they wanted to buy some land. I told them I didn't sell land, but only houses, and sent them to the builder's office, further down the road. When I told Nunn, he was apoplectic, and said that if I had driven down with them I would have earned Marlows ten per cent on the deal. It seemed a very easy way to earn money.

The Plomleys in Maidstone. My father (standing, second from left) with his father (standing, right), his mother (sitting, centre), his five sisters and two of his brothers

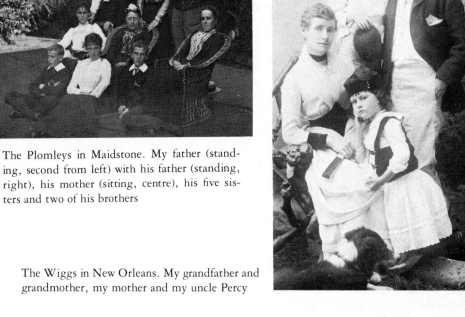

The Wiggs in New Orleans. My grandfather and grandmother, my mother and my uncle Percy

51 Fife Road

Family group in Kingston-upon-Thames. From l. to r., my uncle Percy, my mother with me (aged 15 months) on her knee, my grandfather, my father, Aunt Doll, my grandmother

The author as a small boy

On the day when the matriculation results were to be posted, I went to the university buildings in South Kensington, to know my fate as soon as possible: there was quite a crowd surveying the long alphabetical lists of names. I did not dare look directly for mine, but read upwards through Puseys, Pratts, Potters and Plyfolds until I saw Plomley, Francis Roy. I gave a sigh of relief and bought myself a celebratory cup of coffee.

A drawback to my success was that I should now have to work full-time for Marlows, and I did not look forward to that prospect. The bypass project was gradually being given up as a lost cause, and I was now mostly at the main office. There was no code of conduct restricting the number of agents handling a property, and we three boys were sent round on bicycles, canvassing owners to allow us to place particulars of houses and flats on the firm's books: if possible, we were also to obtain permission to put up a board. Sometimes a house would have the boards of four or five agents in the front garden, which made it a kind of lottery as to which agent a prospective buyer would contact. It was also part of a canvasser's duty to write a description of the premises for use in the office, and I would walk importantly through empty rooms, writing in a notebook, 'Large sitting-room with french doors to well-kept garden' and 'Modern bathroom with h. & c. and usual offices'. It was not demanding work and, because Nunn sat in the office most of the day and wrote out orders-to-view, we had little supervision and made as many or as few calls as we felt like: I was free to meet my friends, or sit on park benches and read.

I had always had ambitions to row, which struck me as a glamorous sport, with the oarsmen leading a pleasantly communal life and swaggering about in brightly-coloured blazers: it was obviously demanding, but the whole mystique appealed to me. I did not have the necessary contacts to join Kingston Rowing Club, so I settled for the Skiff Club. Skiff shoving is probably the most gruelling of aquatic sports, comparable only with galley-slaving, but I found my fellow members to be delightful people, and I spent an enjoyable summer. In the

65

autumn, I answered an advertisement – again in *The Surrey Comet* – inviting membership of a new amateur dramatic society. I interpreted this as the first tiny step towards doing what I really wanted to do.

The society was called the Elmers Players, because it was being run from an address in Avenue Elmers, one of the smarter streets in Surbiton. I was summoned there to meet Captain Toby Grover, a dapper, shy man with a toothbrush moustache and a receding chin. He offered me a cigarette, and asked me if I had done much acting, and I said no, and he asked me if I was interested in the theatre, and I said yes, and then the conversation languished, so he handed me over to his wife, Elma Verity, who had been a professional actress, and who was a volatile lady whose manner, speech and clothes were eminently theatrical. At seventeen, I was difficult to cast, but she took a chance and made me the juvenile lead in *Passing Brompton Road*.

As the son of the house, in the comedy, I was sent for from Oxford to sort out a family difficulty. I did not make my appearance until the beginning of the third act, when I ran on, tossing aside my suitcase and college scarf and saying to the girl who played my sister, 'Here I am, Sis. What's the trouble?' – or words to that effect. Whereupon she took me by the hand and led me downstage to a small table where she sat on a chair on one side and I sat on a chair on the other, and she told me all about it.

It may have been the exhilaration of finding that I could remember my lines, or it could have been the smell of grease-paint or the feel of the lights on my face, but on the first night I decided to indulge in a little creative acting, and I rose from my chair and perched winsomely on the edge of the table, looking down protectively at my sister – whereupon the opposite edge rose up and hit her under the chin. It was the only laugh we got out of *Passing Brompton Road*.

After that, I gave a really diabolical performance as the lawyer, Chesterman, in *Tons of Money*, and then I played another juvenile lead in *The Man from Toronto*, and somewhere in between I played a British Army officer in a maudlin one-acter about a statue of Joan of Arc which comes to life in a French town behind the lines during the Great War – we won a festival with that one – and then I was given the lead in a curious play by Robins Millar called *Thunder in the Air*. It is about a young man named Ronald who had been killed in the war, and then reappears to his family and friends in the guise in which each remembers him – to his father as a ne'er do well, to his fiancée as a romantic lover, to his business partner as a crook, and to his mother as 'clean, white Ronnie'. All in all, it was quite an evening's work. It was a fairly complicated piece of drama in the first place, but it was made all the more so by an actor playing one of the minor characters who cut several pages of exposition near the beginning. There were puzzled faces among our sparse audience at the Hillcroft Theatre, Surbiton.

After only a few months, I had been given the sack from Marlows, and I was not sorry because it was a dreadful dead end. Nunn said he could no longer afford me, and as my wage had risen to only seven-and-sixpence and the commission had proved illusory, the firm must have been in dire straits.

Father suggested that I should tackle the banks and insurance companies, and even managed to produce one or two letters of introduction, but neither these nor my certificate of matriculation made the least impression on the personnel officers who interviewed me. From the questions I was asked, it was obvious that the kind of boy they were looking for was the born leader, the clear-eyed young god who had been captain of rugby, or captain of cricket, or captain of boats, whereas I had never been captain of anything, not even my soul. I have found it generally true that the heroes of my schooldays are now in banks and insurance companies, and having a fairly boring time, whereas those who were the layabouts, like me, are having all the laughs and all the excitement.

Optimistically, I decided to have a shot at theatrical journalism, a highly-skilled craft of which I knew nothing. While at Marlows, I had bluffed my way on to the set of Warner

Brothers film studios at Teddington, and watched the shooting of scenes from a thriller, and I had also got myself taken on for a single unpaid performance in a crowd scene at His Majesty's Theatre, so I wrote amateurish little pieces about those experiences and, not surprisingly, failed to sell them.

My luck changed when I turned out for a game of rugby for the Old Boys one Saturday afternoon. In the changing room I found myself next to Basil de Launay, who had been a contemporary of mine and who was later successful as a financial tycoon in Fleet Street. We exchanged civilities, and he asked me what I was doing. Ruefully, I told him I was doing nothing, and he said he might be able to help. He was in an advertising agency, he said: did I know anything about advertising? I admitted that I didn't, but nevertheless he kindly arranged for me to have an interview with his boss.

Arthur Chadwick was a plump north-countryman whose face was pink and shiny, a fact which he tried to disguise, unsuccessfully, by applying white powder. He had founded Amalgamated Publicity Services Ltd on a capital of five pounds, and built it into a medium-sized West End agency, specializing in direct mail, which is the trade jargon for advertising by post. He read my article on the Warner Brothers studios, asked me a few questions and then invited me to join the firm as a trainee at fifteen shillings a week.

APS was not a smart agency, but it was a workmanlike one. It still had a pinch-penny look, as a hangover from its humble origins, and its offices were in a gloomy sidestreet, shouldered by grimy warehouses and rambling from one building to another. The direct mail side of the business involved the employment of casual labour for addressing envelopes and for matching-in personal greetings on printed letters. The addressing was done by shabby old gentlemen who sat in rows in a large, bare room, scratching away with pen and ink, while the matching-in was done at massed typewriters by pert and sometimes tarty-looking young ladies whose room I had to go through to get to my office, and the concentrated gaze of so much appraising femininity made me keep my eyes to the front.

I began my training as assistant to one of the account executives, an efficient young man named Michael Hughes. His job was to make sure his clients were happy, mainly by reassuring them that all their decisions were the right ones, and by taking off their shoulders all the detailed work involved in administering their advertising.

There was a cheerful bustle about the place, and a healthy, if cynical, belief that nothing which was being done was in the least important. It was pleasant to be surrounded by magazines and periodicals and newspapers of every size, shape and variety, but disappointing that our clients were not the type to buy space in the glossy, expensive and glamorous publications.

The firm's principal client was Spillers Ltd, who are millers and makers of animal foods, and I discovered that Basil de Launay's father was their advertising manager, which made me suspect that I had been hired as a favour, at second remove, to Spillers.

For a few weeks, I made myself generally useful, while learning about the techniques of printing, blockmaking and selling, and then I was given a firm of clients to look after on my own. They were not very important clients, because they bought space in only two publications, *Melody Maker* and *Rhythm*, neither of which charged much for it. They were two affable Jews known as the Lewin Brothers, and they ran a musical instruments shop, off Charing Cross Road, catering for the dance band trade. I visited them once a month and, over a cup of tea in the back room, we made a jigsaw assembly of pictures of trumpets, clarinets and saxophones for their next advertisements. Sometimes we were joined by customers, who were also affable and Jewish, and all of whom favoured very smart suits indeed. On one occasion I met Max Bacon, drummer and comedy vocalist with the celebrated Ambrose orchestra, who was the most affable and Jewish of them all. An advantage in looking after the Lewin Brothers advertising was that voucher copies of the dance band papers used to arrive on my desk, and I began to take an interest in the world of popular music and jazz.

One day, Hughes showed me a small order which had come in for some promotion for the Showman's Club, which was about to open in the West End. He was going round to look at the place, and would I care to go with him? I jumped at the opportunity. In my mind a showman meant a man of the theatre – men like Cochran and Charlot were showmen – and I imagined that the club would be full of glamorous and influential actors, actresses, managers, designers, agents . . . all the people who could further my ambitions.

The club turned out to be a single small room, high up in an office building, with a few tables and chairs and a bar. It was empty except for the manager and the barman, but then it had not got going yet; in fact, the first concern was to get members. 'How much is the subscription?' I asked. For founder members, it was to be a very modest sum. And what were the qualifications for membership? Here the manager appeared a little vague. 'May I join?' I asked, diffidently. He appeared delighted. I filled in a form, putting down my profession as 'actor' – well, it was only a matter of time, I thought.

I began going to the club regularly at lunchtime, but I did not keep up my attendances for long; the place was nearly always empty, and such fellow members as I did encounter were indeed showmen, but of a kind whose influence would be of little use to me – they were all from the fairground and the pin-table arcade.

Having been given a chance to try my hand at designing layouts and writing copy, I was moved into the production department, which was the creative hub of the agency. At that time, it consisted of only two people, Denis Bullough, a gifted visualiser with a quiet and impish manner, and Basil de Launay. Between them they devised all the press advertisements, leaflets, broadsides, mailing shots, catalogues, booklets and whatever. Attached to the department were seven or eight artists who made finished drawings which went to the block-makers, but as the studio was not big enough to accommodate them all, two of them worked in the production department office. One was a young Burmese with the economical name of Ba On. He lived an unconventional life, and it was scarcely a matter for comment when, for his own good reason, he arrived one morning dressed as a matador. The other was a tall, loose-limbed cynical man named Mickey Marston, who was in his thirties and had served on the Western Front during the war. He hated responsibility, and claimed that the only worthwhile occupation was the bruised fruit business, in which one bought one's stock in the morning, sold as much as possible, and threw the rest away because it would be inedible the next day. In moments of stress, I often think of the attractions of the bruised fruit business.

Every morning, I was given job-sheets for the day's work. I might be called upon for something dreary, such as providing layouts and copy for small advertisements in country news-papers for Spillers Chick Foods, or it might be copy for a booklet about women's hairdressing, or an article for a house magazine, or the provision of ideas on how to sell a new product which showed no obvious advantages over a dozen similar ones already on the market. Many of the jobs were amusing, and some of them were challenging. As the youngest and least experienced – in just about every way – I was given jobs which older members of the staff thought would be good for me, such as bringing up to date a catalogue of birth control appliances and sex aids marketed by a morose Indian. I was on frequent call as a model for the firm's primitive photographic studio, which had been set up in the basement and, as I was reasonably husky, it was my job to escort the aged accountant to and from Barclay's Bank every morning. As my skill at drawing left much to be desired, I began to attend weekly life classes in an attic in New Oxford Street at the modest cost of one-and-sixpence an evening.

APS was not big enough to justify running a staff canteen so, at one o'clock, we scattered. The best value in the district was at Poggiolli's, in Charlotte Street. On the ground floor, you could order a plate of minestrone for 3d which, with a demi-spaghetti at 4d, a piece of bread for 1d, and 1d for the waiter, totalled only 9d. Upstairs, it was more expensive; there were tablecloths, and one was expected to leave the waiter 2d.

In a basement in Denmark Street was a Chinese restaurant called the Nanking, where one had a set lunch of curried fish, chicken chop suey, a spring roll and rice, and finished with lychees and a pot of jasmine tea, and it was all for one-and-sixpence. For about the same money, one could climb the marble staircase to the first floor of the Tottenham Court Road Corner House, where an orchestra of a dozen or more black-jacketed musicians played light classics and dance tunes. Here, in opulent surroundings and sitting in an upholstered chair, I could order cold steak-and-kidney pie for ninepence, a vegetable for 3d, a pudding for 4d, leave 2d for the waitress, and send up my card to the orchestra leader, who bowed politely in my direction as he raised his baton to conduct my request. I was particularly fond of the Lizst Second Hungarian Rhapsody.

I spent many lunch-hours in Foyles Bookshop, which was then a much more exciting place than it is now, because it dealt extensively in secondhand books and there were many bargains to be picked up. Messrs W. & G. Foyle Ltd took over from the station bookstall and W. Cooper & Son in furthering my literary education. If I lunched on a cheese roll and a cup of tea, then I could afford to buy a secondhand book. Another lunchtime haunt was Imhof's, where sometimes there were free record recitals.

A relic of APS days is my devotion to the *New Yorker*. Five magazines were required reading for creative men and women in the advertising business: the *New Yorker*, which was smart, brittle, laconic and up-to-the-minute, the *Saturday Evening Post*, which was homey, corny and standing for all the reactionary attitudes of small-town America, *Gebrauchsgraphik*, a German monthly devoted to all that was new in commercial art and design, and the two trade papers, the *Advertiser's Weekly* and *World's Press News*.

In the 1930s, the *New Yorker* was at its brilliant and irreverent peak, with such contributors as Robert Benchley, Dorothy Parker, Alexander Woollcott, James Thurber and Peter Arno, all drilled and cajoled by the great editor, Harold Ross. I admired especially the style of the four or five pages of comment and gossip which open the magazine under the heading 'Talk of the Town', and it was my ambition, one day, to write as amusingly, as clearly and succinctly as this weekly co-operative effort. In an attempt to indoctrinate myself, I subscribed for many years, until I found that I was accumulating hundreds of back numbers which I would never have time to read, and I decided that if my style had not been influenced by then it never would be.

Summer evenings were spent on the river, either training for skiff regattas or just messing about in boats. The Thames was peaceful then because almost all the craft were propelled by hand. Many river-lovers kept their own boats, which were looked after for them at one of the boathouses, or one could hire a punt, dinghy, skiff or canoe by the hour, at one and sixpence for the first hour and a shilling per hour thereafter.

For wooing, a punt was best, because there was room for two to lie side by side on the cushions; in fact, it was possible to halve the expense, because the craft was long enough for two couples. For privacy, one asked for a punt with a cover, which was of green canvas and could be drawn down over iron stanchions, enveloping the occupants in a cool green twilight. When asking the boatman for a punt with a cover, while accompanied by a lady, it was customary to conceal one's intentions by looking up at the clear blue sky and saying, 'It looks as if it could rain, Jim. Don't you think?', and Jim, who was well schooled in this manoeuvre would reply, 'Ar, it does that, sir', and never the ghost of a wink was exchanged.

A covered punt was also ideal for camping, although it was advisable to do the cooking on dry land. During my second summer of skiff shoving, soon after I joined APS, I hired a punt for a week during my summer holiday. I was on my own, but did a great deal of entertaining. I had just acquired my first serious girlfriend — at least, I was serious even if she was not: her name was Monica, she was three years older than I, she worked at the Hong Kong and Shanghai Bank, and she ran a small car. She, too, was on holiday, so we spent our days gliding up and down the reach from Hampton Court to Teddington. One day I invited Dennis Bullough, Ba On and Basil de Launay to come down to Kingston when they left the office and spend the night aboard. We moored off Stephen's Ait, and did not bed down until about 3.00 am. As a result, we did not wake up until fairly late, and we found that the preparation of a cooked breakfast for four on a primus stove takes a long time, so Bullough went ashore to telephone APS and tell them they would have to do without a production department until midday.

A near-essential for a punt was a portable gramophone and an album of records. For such a peaceful means of transport, sweet music was called for, and sentimental tunes by Ambrose and his Orchestra, and songs by such crooners as Cliff Edwards and Gene Austin sounded delightful when heard across the water. It was only when you were homeward bound and were paddling or poling quite hard to get back to the boathouse before your next hour was up that you put on such encouraging sounds as the bands of Louis Armstrong or Frankie Trumbauer.

The skiff racing world was – and is – very small, as there were – and are – only three or four clubs participating, of which the Skiff Club is the senior. The regatta season is in the late summer, after the best-boat regattas are over, and we would then be joined by quite a number of rowing men. The regattas were informal affairs and after the main events of the day there would be gondola races, between six-men crews standing in a punt, using long paddles, and scratch canoe races in Rob-Roy fours. It was not uncommon, for one reason or another, to end the afternoon in the river, before starting the evening's consumption of Hodgson's bitter at eightpence a pint.

On fifteen shillings a week, some of which had to go on fares and lunches, it was obviously difficult for me to be a satisfactory swain so far as Monica was concerned. In an

74

attempt to, as it were, bring her down to my level, I suggested that she should join the Skiff Club, which she did, and it was there that she met the man who is now her husband. It just goes to show the truth of the old Cockney saying that you should never introduce your donah to a pal.

However, teenage hearts are soon mended and, anyway, I transferred my allegiance from the Skiff Club to Kingston Rowing Club, which then occupied a clubhouse on Raven's Ait. Right next door was Surbiton Swimming Club, and there I met Jean, one of the prettiest girls I have ever seen, with corn-coloured hair, a cream-and-roses complexion, bright blue eyes and a tip-tilted nose.

There are disadvantages in having to do one's wooing under the surveillance of fellow members of a rowing club, and I would blush furiously when, as the junior eight paddled past the Swimming Club, there would be megaphoned instructions from the coach for 'Two' to keep his eyes in the boat and his mind on the job. It was a very happy summer, rowing every evening, escorting Jean home afterwards, spending Saturdays at regattas and Sundays lazing in a punt or sunbathing on the ait. Alas, Jean and I were together for only a few months, and I confess that our parting was all my fault.

The following spring, a blow fell. APS had made the mistake of putting all its eggs in one basket, and when their one major client, Spillers, decided to take their advertising elsewhere, heads had to fall. My head was one of them, and once again I was faced with finding a job in the depths of a trade depression. As an advertising man, the obvious way to set about it seemed to be by advertising, so I wrote a sales letter about myself, paid APS to print it in facsimile typewriting, and arranged for a matched-in copy to be sent to the creative chief of every advertising agency in London. I then sat back and awaited results.

To say the least, they were disappointing; they consisted of a few polite acknowledgments of my letter, and a four-page printed form from an agency called Greenly's, which I kept for years because it epitomised all that was idiotic and pretentious in the advertising business. It asked for the answers to over a hundred questions – one of which was, did I have poise? – plus an autobiographical sketch from 500 to 1000 words in length. Greenlys did not offer to pay for the day's work entailed in doing all this, and must have wasted considerable sums in employing someone to read the stuff – if, indeed, it was ever read.

Eventually, I was given a job by the Shaw Publishing Company, which issued a group of trade papers and some singularly dull reference books from a drab, stone-passaged building in Carmelite Street. I was to look after the classified advertisements printed in the back pages of the *Furnishing Record, Business* and the *Advertiser's Weekly*.

The fact that the firm paid minimal wages may have accounted for the sullen gloom which clouded the faces of the employees, but the wretched accommodation must also have had something to do with it. I shared a small, airless office with two others. When I say 'airless' I mean it literally; there was no window, and the only daylight we saw was when a door of an adjoining office was opened. I was paid thirty shillings a week, which was to be increased by five shillings if I succeeded in pushing up the revenue by fifteen per cent, by ten shillings if I increased it by twenty-five per cent, and a reckless thirty shillings if I doubled it and kept it doubled for not less than two months. After a few weeks, during which the revenue showed no sign of going up by even one per cent, I lost interest and was happy to get the sack, being so eager to get out of the place that I asked that the usual week's notice should be dispensed with. (I hope I have not been too hard on this sad organization because I have just realized that these lines are being scribbled on the blank pages of a dummy copy of *Who's Who in Congregationalism*, which I seem to have abstracted from their offices all those years ago. I feel a twinge of conscience is called for.)

One of the members of the Elmers Players was a gaunt, rather eccentric young man who was even more stagestruck than I was: he thought, read and dreamed theatre, all the time.

His name was, and is, Raymond Mander and, after a longish spell as an actor, he became co-proprietor of the Raymond Mander and Joe Mitchenson Theatre Collection, which is now one of our national assets. He brought along to rehearsals a striking young woman named Aileen Street who was, without a doubt, one of the most brilliant and exceptional people I have ever met. She was six years older than I, had huge brown eyes, a mop of brown hair, a full figure and many talents. She was a good actress, an accomplished singer, a first-rate pianist, a well-versed cellist, a most skilled water-colourist, a competent writer and, given a piece of inexpensive material, a needle, thimble and scissors, she could produce within an hour or two a dress of which a professional couturier would not be ashamed. She also spoke fluent French and was a good cook. I found her irresistible.

I owe a great deal to Aileen; she taught me much about life and about people and about the arts and about myself. It was comforting, too, that there was never any question of my not being able to keep up with her financially; she was always as broke as I was.

She persuaded her father to finance her to study in the opera class at the Royal College of Music and with Richard Temple Savage, who was also a student, she evolved a scheme to present a single performance of Mozart's *Il Seraglio (Die Ent-führung aus dem Serail)* at the college's Parry Opera Theatre during the Easter vacation. The opera was something of a rarity in those days, and there was no set of orchestral parts available, so Richard copied the whole lot, a massive task which took him many days and nights.

Casting presented no problems: Aileen would sing Constanza, Margaret Field-Hyde would sing Blonda, I would play the non-singing part of The Bashaw, and an excellent young tenor named Peter Pears would be the handsome hero, Belmonte. Richard was confident that he could raise the necessary thirty or so orchestral players from among his colleagues, and he would conduct. Aileen would design the scenery, which we would all help to build and paint, and would design and make all the costumes; she would also direct.

A really serious difficulty was getting a chorus together. There are only two chorus items in the opera, and the appearances are too short to be interesting, but Richard had the brilliant idea that the ladies of the seraglio should be played by boys, and he borrowed the choir of a South London school. Musically, the effect was delightful; Aileen dressed them in cheerfully grotesque costumes, and they were one of the hits of the evening. To fill the stage further, some stalwart rugby-playing friends were persuaded to strip off and coat themselves with a sticky mixture of yellow ochre and Guinness: they made most convincing Ethiopian slaves.

The dress rehearsal was set for the morning of the performance, and both Aileen and I missed it. The amount of work that she, Richard and I put in was enormous. Having worked flat out for days, Aileen and I sat up most of the night making last minute adjustments to costumes and properties. We lay down for a few hours sleep and woke up in the middle of the morning, with the realization that the rehearsal must be half over: in fact, the musicians were putting away their instruments when we arrived. It had obviously been a scratch rehearsal with two of the principals missing, and the rest of the cast reacted with varying degrees of resignation and frustration. As I made-up that evening, I realised that I had never rehearsed some of my dialogue scenes at all.

As the college authorities would not allow us to charge for admission or to take a collection, we paid for the enterprise by putting an advertisement in the *Daily Telegraph*, offering free tickets to all comers but suggesting that voluntary contributions would be welcome. We paid back an initial float of twenty-five pounds borrowed from Aileen's parents and just about covered expenses.

It was at about that time that I left Kingston. My father's business had been seriously effected by the slump, by the competition of the big chain stores, who could offer toilet articles and cosmetics at rock-bottom prices, and by the fact that another pharmacist had opened just a few doors away, which was sheer foolishness because there was not trade enough for one shop, let alone two. For nearly thirty-five years, Father had conducted a quiet, rather old-fashioned business; now, sadly, he tried to compete with the brash methods of his rivals. He began using a home printing press, festooning the shop with erratically-printed little posters, bearing such phrases as 'A REAL LIVER ROUSER, 1/6d'. But the new approach was of little use: he was 65, he was losing money, and the only solution was to let the shop – if he could find a tenant in such a time of depressed trade – and take temporary jobs as a locum.

We moved to Trinity Road, Wimbledon, where he rented the upper flat in a Victorian house for twenty-five shillings a week. There were two rooms for me on the top floor, where I could have a degree of independence. It was nearly eighteen months before he was able to let the shop and the living accommodation above to an occulist, by which time, despite extreme economies, most of his capital had gone. Locum jobs were rare, but occasionally he would set off for some provincial town to spend a week or two in digs, and bring home a few much-needed pounds.

My few weeks with the Shaw Publishing Company had not been entirely wasted, because I had taken the opportunity of inserting a few unpaid advertisements of my own, of the 'Young man, go anywhere, do anything for God's sake get me out of here' variety. There were two replies which seemed worth investigating. One was from a man named Acker, who wanted me to go and live in his house in Lincolnshire and help him write a book. He took me out for a meal and talked at length about his ideas, the main one being that the only way for Britain to get out of her economic troubles was to persuade the Prince of Wales to take over as dictator. I was grateful for the meal but declined the offer, telling him that my interest in politics was minimal. The second was from a man named W. F. Mitchell who asked if I would be interested in an advertising job in the Channel Islands.

I went to see him, and he told me that he proposed to start

a business in Jersey, selling horoscopes by post. He had been running a similar business in Copenhagen, but I gathered that he had run into a little trouble with the Danish postal authorities, and a move had been thought advisable: however, he had discovered that Jersey had a certain amount of autonomy in postal matters, and things should be all right there. He wanted someone to lay out his press advertisements, write sales letters and promotion material, and make himself generally useful, and he offered me four pounds a week. It was twice as much money as I had yet earned, the proposition sounded amusing, it was spring and I liked the idea of going to Jersey, so I accepted.

Born in Canada, but an American citizen, Mitchell was in his late sixties: he had been a Methodist preacher, a trick cyclist, the proprietor of Rector's night clubs in London and Paris, a director of London's first *palais de danse* in Hammersmith, and the man to bring the first American jazz band to this country. Now it was horoscopes.

When I arrived in Jersey, the action had already begun. He had rented the first floor of a new building in the centre of St Helier, above the extensive shop premises of Burtons the Tailors, and carpenters were at work erecting partitions and installing large nests of pigeon holes. Crates of office stuff had been shipped from Copenhagen, and a suspicious customs officer was inspecting it as it was unpacked. Duplicating machines, typewriters and desks were being hauled up the stairs, and Mitchell's blonde lady companion was hiring girls as office staff and offering them fifteen shillings a week, which was the going rate on the island.

In the midst of it all, Mitchell was planning his campaign. The Copenhagen astrologer had been called Hasan Karan; the new one would be called Professor El-Tanah, and if we depicted him in an Indian turban against a background of the pyramids, then we would be featuring two sectors of the mysterious east on one letterhead.

Advertisements were inserted in women's twopenny weeklies, in motion picture fan magazines, and in other periodicals designed for what Humbert Wolfe called 'the damp souls of housemaids'. To demonstrate his ability to divine character and forecast the future from the stars, Professor El-Tanah offered a free, trial astrological reading. All you had to do was send the date and place of your birth, together with threepence in stamps. In those days, threepence was quite a lot of money, but nobody ever queried the semantic discrepancy between threepence and free, and pretty soon we were up to our necks in threepences. In return for that sum, our correspondent received a three-page general reading applying to those born under whichever of the twelve birth signs was relevant. With it went a letter from the Professor saying that while making these preliminary calculations he had seen that something very important was going to happen to his correspondent in the near future, and that he would have liked to have gone ahead and made detailed reckonings, but unfortunately the pressures on his time were such that this was not possible; if, however, the modest sum of two pounds was sent to him, then he would cast a complete individual reading giving full knowledge of that important event and all other future eventualities. Postal orders and cheques began to flow in.

Individual readings were assembled by means of a book of astronomical tables called an ephemeris; when a particular date is looked up, the positions of the sun, the moon and the planets are shown, and there was a duplicated sheet of material for each variation. A set of the sheets was taken from their pigeon holes, stapled together in a fancy cover and sent off. It was, in essence, a handmade version of the computerised horoscopes which are on sale today.

The material was written by a genuine astrologer; I never met him, nor even knew his name, but I was told that he lived in Paris and that he had originally prepared it all in Hasan Karan days. It was cleverly and positively written, and anyone who believed in it and acted on the advice which was given was getting good value for money. In every case, the main message was: *Have confidence in yourself. Don't worry. The conjunction of the stars at the time of your birth shows plainly that you have the powers to make more of your life, so go forward. Do not be held back by fears. You have an attractive personality, so do not give way to feelings of inferiority.* There was also some good common sense about looking after one's health. I am sure we had many satisfied customers.

One of my earliest jobs was to write a complete issue of a little magazine called *Twentieth Century Astrology*, which we used as an envelope-stuffer and sent in all directions. The main feature was an exclusive interview with Professor El-Tanah, *'a lithe, brown-skinned figure of medium height, dressed in neat European clothes and with a perpetual charming smile which discloses two rows of incredibly white teeth.'* It revealed that for five years the Professor had been studying, calculating and planning in his little villa in the South of France and, with the aid of astrological charts he had compiled, the calculations necessary to cast individual horoscopes could now be halved. *'I'm going to tell every man and woman in Great Britain how they can remodel their lives and achieve success, prosperity and happiness by a knowledge of what the stars foretell.'* When asked why he had chosen Jersey as the centre of his operations, the Professor replied, *'Firstly, sunshine; secondly, clarity of atmosphere for observational purposes; thirdly, peace and quiet to enable me to get down to work.'* He then showed his interviewer his *'splendidly equipped little laboratory'*, which was, of course, quite fictitious, but which was drawn-in on an illustration of the Burton building. Dome-shaped, with a telescope emerging from the top, it looked quite impressive. This article became celebrated, in its way, because it was quoted *in extenso* in *John Bull* and the other aggressive weekly magazines which 'exposed' and attacked the Professor and urged their readers to have nothing to do with his enterprise.

I enjoyed Jersey. It is extraordinary to find such a wide variety of beautiful scenery, ranging from rugged Cornish-style coastline to the small-scale charm of Surrey, in an area only eight miles by ten – and then there were the eminently sensible licensing laws, and excellent bitter at only fourpence a pint. I had decided to live cheaply and try to save money and, indeed, such a project was possible. I started by renting a room on the top floor of a terrace house in Pomona Road. There was no electricity or gas, so I had to make do with candlelight, and the lavatory was two floors down and then along the garden path, but I was paying only eight shillings a week, and that included having my bed made and my room dusted. For my food, I relied on very cheap little restaurants near the harbour. Aileen came over for a weekend and read me the riot act, because she was a staunch advocate of health foods, and here was I living on chocolate biscuits and meat pies. She scrubbed out the chamber pot, which was one of the few amenities provided, and announced that from now on it was my salad bowl, and that salad and fruit and cheese were to form a major part of my diet.

An event I remember with affection was a visit by the O'Mara Opera Company, on what must have been one of its last tours. In a two-week season at the Springfield Theatre, they played fourteen different operas. They had two sets of scenery, indoors and outdoors, and an orchestra of only five, but it was opera sung by an experienced, if elderly, company, and Jersey should have been grateful, but the audiences were sadly sparse.

One Sunday morning, I got up early and went on a day's excursion to St Malo. It was my first visit to France.

I was fascinated by the beautiful old town, and walked the narrow, cobbled streets with joy, exploring the little shops and cafés. It was a feast day, and intricate designs in coloured sand had been laid on the streets to be trodden by a religious procession. In the church tower was a bell which boomed so loudly that it seemed to shake the place. I wandered on the top of the wide town wall in the sunshine, looking down on the Place Châteaubriand, with its three big cafés, each fronted by a pattern of circular metal tables and their attendant chairs. It was hot and wonderful — and I spent the afternoon in a cinema! I know it sounds like madness to spend half of one's very first day in France sitting in a darkened auditorium staring at shadows, but films were important in my life and I wanted the experience of seeing a film in French, without English subtitles, and I wanted to see if a French cinema was any different to an English one. (Except for having to pay to use the lavatory, it seemed the same.) Looking back, the one thing that does strike me as odd about my behaviour is the programme I chose to see: somewhere in St Malo there must have been French films showing, but the double feature I saw consisted of dubbed versions of Korda's *The Private Life of Henry VIII* and Douglas Fairbanks's *Around the World in Eighty Minutes*, both of which I had already seen in the original versions.

Aileen came to Jersey for a month or two during the college vacation, and we moved to furnished rooms in Havre des Pas. They cost twenty-five shillings a week, but they were spacious and comfortable. I remember that summer as one of blistering heat. We explored the island together at weekends, and on other days she sat on the beach in the sun until she was almost black. We made the down payment on a bicycle for our mutual use.

When she returned to England, she went to join her father who was visiting the Malvern Festival. I telephoned her there, and someone at the hotel told me that she had been taken ill and was in a nursing home, but my informant did not know which one. It was worrying, and it seemed to me that I should go to see if she was all right. I was not sure if I had enough money for the fare to Malvern, so I set off on the boat to Weymouth with our bicycle. I had never before owned a bicycle (or even half one, as in this case) and had done remarkably little cycling, so I think I did rather well to complete ninety-three miles overnight.

From Weymouth I rode to Yeovil. The reason why I made Yeovil my first objective, apart from the fact that it is on as direct a route as any, was because on a West Country camping holiday with a rowing club friend the summer before, we had stopped at the Mermaid Hotel for a meal. Our waitress had been a ravishingly pretty girl, with dark hair and an olive skin, whose low-cut dress revealed the upper slopes of what seemed to be a pair of perfect breasts. Although I had spoken no words

84

to her other than my decision on whether to take roast potatoes or mashed, I had remembered her from time to time, and I thought it would be pleasant to catch another glimpse of her. I had neither the time nor the money to dine at the Mermaid, but I looked in for half a pint of beer and put my head round the dining-room door to see if she was on duty, but it was either her evening off or she had moved on to display her charms elsewhere.

From Yeovil, I took a train to Bath, and then cycled from Bath to Malvern. When I arrived, early in the morning, I was so tired that I fell off. I went to a telephone box and asked the operator to help me by giving me a list of all the nursing homes, and began ringing round. I soon found the one where Aileen was and rushed to visit her, to discover that she had completely recovered from whatever minor ailment had smitten her, and that my journey had been quite unnecessary.

Her father, a solicitor, asked me to lunch. He must have sensed immediately that I had little to offer his daughter in any material way but, at any rate, there seemed to be devotion, so he was kind enough to invite me to stay for a few days to keep her company. I was a little put-out to notice in the hotel register that one of my hated rivals had been a member of the party during the weekend, but as a guest it would have been impolite to have started a quarrel.

With autumn approaching, I decided that I had had enough of astrology. I had been in Jersey four months and did not want to stay away from Aileen any longer, nor did I relish the idea of a winter in the Channel Islands. Besides, the joke was over.

I was not in Mitchell's confidence regarding the financial progress of the business, but there was no doubt that the daily take was a very considerable one. He was employing translators, and advertisements would soon appear in French and German. He was already tackling the American market, and the first three replies had reached us in response to an advertisement in a local newspaper in the corn belt: two of them were from unmarried mothers-to-be, and the third from a farmer who complained that his neighbour was bewitching his cattle.

I went to Mitchell and told him I was leaving. He seemed genuinely sorry and said that if I stayed with him I should be making a lot of money within a few years. This was quite untrue, because nobody was to make any money except himself: three or four years later, he absconded, leaving debts all over the island and his staff unpaid. He was heard of briefly in Paris and then disappeared.

When I reached London, I borrowed twenty-five pounds from my father, who could have ill-afforded to lend me even twenty-five shillings, had some letterheads printed – F. Roy Plomley, Advertising Consultant. 'From a handbill to a whole campaign' – and set about trying to get some freelance jobs. I also got in touch with a girl named Joyce, whom I had met in Jersey and who had done some crowd work in films. I had told her of my ambition to get into some branch of the entertainment business, and had suggested that this might be my way in. She had promised to introduce me to her agent, which she did.

In fact, one could register with as many of the smaller agents as one wished. The procedure was simple: one filled in a form giving particulars of age (approximate), height (more or less), colouring (actual), professional experience (real or imagined) and available wardrobe (what one had, or thought one could borrow). The form was then attached to a suitably flattering photograph and put into a drawer in the filing cabinet.

At about six o'clock in the evening, when the production staffs at the studios had assessed their needs for the next day, crowd artists used to run round to the agents' offices to see if there was any hope of an engagement. The rumour that a certain agent was handling a large call brought people surging up the stairs, usually to be met by a bored clerk or a cheeky office boy who would say that those needed had already been chosen, and would everybody else stop blocking the bloody passage.

A great deal of crowd work was channelled through the Film

86

Artists Association, which one joined by paying a subscription of half-a-crown a month, and which maintained a casting office and club rooms in Soho. The rooms were gloomy and vast, and comprised lounges, bars both for drinks and snacks, a restaurant and a card room. There was a seedy air about the premises, but the members radiated a friendly warmth. From early morning, the place was filled with elderly unemployed actors and actresses, resting chorus boys and girls, models, layabouts and 'types'.

Occasionally, the casting director or his assistant would come upstairs from the office and wander among us, looking for members who would fill the bill for a call from a studio for twenty-five convicts, sixteen genteel old ladies, fifty evening dress diners or forty miscellaneous Latins. The etiquette was to ignore him while he was prowling, but everyone was careful to show him the better profile and to act nonchalantly. If he could not find enough of the types he was looking for on the premises, he would descend to his office to complete the list by telephoning. There was a scratchy loudspeaker on the wall and, towards the end of the day, his voice would announce the names of the lucky ones who would be working the next day. 'Casting Office calling. The following are wanted at BIP on *McGlusky the Sea Rover* tomorrow morning at eight o'clock. . .'

I had been a member for about three weeks when the casting director stopped beside me for the first time.

'Working tomorrow?'

'Er – no.'

'Would you mind losing that moustache?' He referred to a thin adornment of the Ronald Colman pattern which I wore at that time.

'No.'

'Be down at Shepherd's Bush at five o'clock tomorrow afternoon. It's a location call for *Brown on Resolution*. Get yourself fitted for a sailor's uniform at Nathan's.'

I was to make my professional debut.

4

Having changed into naval uniform at the Gaumont-British studios in Shepherd's Bush, I was taken by motor-coach to Holborn Viaduct station where I spent the night as one of a party of ratings which, times without number, was marched on to a platform and entrained, whereupon the camera moved in on the star, John Mills, who leaned out of a carriage window to bid farewell to his co-star, Betty Balfour. The director was Walter Forde, who liked to relax on the set by playing the piano, and his little foible had been pandered to by having a grand piano unloaded on to the platform.

The title of the film, from a novel by C. S. Forester, was later changed to *Forever England*, as it was thought that the original title sounded too much like a dissertation on moral values by a theologian named Brown.

The following week, I was at Elstree, playing a Young Turk in a film called *Abdul the Damned*. It was directed by Karl Grune, produced by Max Schach, photographed by Karl Freund, and starred Fritz Kortner and Nils Asther; it was, of course, a British film. A month later, I was an 18th-century Swedish revolutionary in *The Dictator*, which was directed by Victor Saville and starred Clive Brook and Madeleine Carroll, who was beautiful. I was involved in an attack on Miss Carroll's coach, and Mr Brook leapt to her rescue with such spirit that he knocked out one of the teeth of the man who was next to me.

The work fascinated me. I loved the sights and sounds and smells of the studios. I enjoyed watching the technical rituals of the camera crew and sound recordists and electricians. I studied every move made by the actors and, when possible, stationed myself behind the director, so that I could watch the scene from his viewpoint. I trespassed into scene docks and plaster shops, and was a ready listener to every anecdote, complaint, piece of gossip or scrap of information that was available.

There were two schools of thought among crowd artists on how to make oneself wanted the following day. Some said it was better to keep out of the camera's range whenever possible; others claimed that to have appeared in the foreground meant that you were likely to be wanted on succeeding days for continuity reasons. My policy was to get in view whenever I could because there was always the chance that a director would single me out for an odd line, and then be so impressed by my delivery of it that he would promote me to a sizeable role. I realised that such a thing had probably never happened in the history of film-making – but there had to be a first time for everything. I learned that one had to have confidence, too: there was the occasion during the making of *The Dictator* when Victor Saville called to the crowd, 'I want somebody to shout out "To the Palace!" ' – and by the time I had screwed up my courage to do so, somebody else had got in with the line, and thereby earned himself an extra ten shillings. I'll swear he didn't shout it nearly as well as I would have done!

The pay for crowd work was miserable – one guinea a day. For that, one had to be at Elstree, Teddington, Shepperton or Beaconsfield at eight o'clock in the morning and work until seven-thirty in the evening. After that, overtime was paid at half-a-crown an hour. Fares took a sizeable piece out of the guinea, and in addition there was commission to be paid to the agent or the FAA. If exterior scenes were to be filmed and the weather was not right, the studio was entitled to pay you off with five shillings and send you home again.

It was not surprising that fiddles flourished. I never felt

inclined to try any of them myself – nor, indeed, did I have the opportunity – but a popular one involved two adjoining studios at Elstree. There were many who boasted of having signed on at one of them and then climbed the fence and signed on at the other, thus having two pay-chits at the end of the day. It was at one of those two studios, where I was playing an English soldier in a film about the Black-and-Tans, that I saw among the other khaki-clad figures the man who had booked me for the job: the crowd casting manager had cast himself in his own crowd!

If one was not chosen for a call, one could always go to the studio 'on the if-it' ('If-it' works, you're lucky!). Inevitably, if the call was large, there were a few artists who did not turn up because they had found something more profitable to do, so the idea was to present yourself as a substitute for one of the missing bodies. I remember trying it at Ealing without success, but it worked at Twickenham, where an affable assistant director named Jimmy Davidson took me on for a couple of night's work on a film called *Last Journey*.

Twickenham was a sausage-machine studio, where cheaply-made pictures were produced two-at-a-time. When the schedule had been worked-out for the making of a film by day, a couple of writers would be hired to devise another film which could use the same sets for the same length of time, and this would be made at night with a different cast and a different set of technicians.

There were about 5,000 cinemas in the United Kingdom, and a constant need to fill screen-time cheaply. I heard of one producer who made travelogues by photographing picture postcards, provided a musical background by playing the organ himself, and spoke his own commentary.

There was no work for me at all at the turn of the year, and December and January were blank months. I did one or two small advertising jobs and filled in some time by acting as business manager for *An Evening of Chamber Music* at the Conway Hall. Aileen sang some songs by Debussy, Schubert's 'Das Hird auf den Felsen', and some she had composed herself, with

Richard Savage playing the clarinet and Charles Groves (now Sir Charles Groves, CBE and ex-Music Director of the English National Opera) at the piano. A group of instrumentalists assembled by Richard played Beethoven's Septet in E flat and Schubert's Octet in F. There was no expectation of making a profit, and the performers contributed towards the expenses.

I had introduced Raymond Mander to the FAA and sometimes we would make a tour of the agents' offices together. A bond we had was collecting theatricalia, although he was much more serious about it than I was. We would make sorties into junk shops or second-hand bookshops, each taking a corner, and emerge covered with dust and cobwebs and clutching battered copies of actors' memoirs or bundles of old programmes, which we bought for a few coppers.

There was plenty of time for reading while sitting in the FAA and sometimes, if the weather discouraged a walk to break the monotony and there were no friends around, the boredom could be extreme. One day I came across a concert party pianist who had somehow acquired the sheet music of what must, without exception, be the worst comic song ever published, and he was playing it over on the battered upright piano used for occasional dances held in the evenings. It was called 'When I met Charlie in a Chalk Pit', and it really was as horrible as its title. Just because there was nothing else to do, we learned it by heart.

February brought one day's work as a French student in a patriotic picture called *Royal Cavalcade*, and the following month I put in a few days and nights on a costume film called *Drake of England*. In it, I appeared in several different roles, but nobody seemed to mind. I began as one of Drake's archers, and we spent some nights sacking a South American city which had been built in a field in Elstree. We then moved to a tributary of the Thames near Shepperton, where the *Golden Hind* came to anchor and the crew rowed ashore to be greeted by none other than Her Majesty Queen Elizabeth I, played by Flora Robson or Athene Seyler, or one of the other ladies who were in the Queen Elizabeth business at that time. I also appeared as one of the locals cheering the Queen, and I am not sure that I was not one of the men-at-arms holding back the cheering locals as well. Another of my roles, as a Spanish seaman, was downright dangerous.

This was another night sequence. We were told to climb up onto a wheeled platform, some fifteen feet high. In front of us was a section of ship's rail, and behind us was the camera. We all held long spars and, when the director blew a whistle, a serried rank of stagehands pushed our platform forward, at the same time that someone set fire to the hulk of a ship which had been built on the grass in front of us. The intended impression was of us Spaniards desperately trying to fend off a fireship which was drifting towards us. It did not work that way because some idiot had filled the fireship with cutting-room waste, and when a torch was thrown into it there was not a fire but a flare-up. The sturdy men below us, bowed to their work, could not see what was going on, and continued to push us into the flames. All we could do was protect our faces with our hands and throw ourselves down on the deck. One man jumped to the ground and damaged his leg. All that was seen on the screen were frightened silhouettes against a blinding white inferno.

In May came a singing job. Gaumont-British were to stage a large-scale patriotic scena for a week at their cinemas in Shepherd's Bush and Hammersmith and, as I had naturally listed singing among my accomplishments when registering with agents, I was despatched to sing to T. C. Fairbairn, the producer of the annual season of *Hiawatha* at the Royal Albert Hall, who was to stage the scena. I sang my one audition song, 'When a maiden takes your fancy', from *Il Seraglio* and, to my surprise, was stopped after the first verse and engaged. Perhaps it would be fair to add that I had had five singing lessons, in the hope of just such an eventuality. I would have taken more, but I was only able to pay for them when I was working, and I had not been working all that much. I had also had one or two free ones, kindly given me by Aileen. (Incidentally, she and I had now broken up, as had been inevitable in view of the difference in our ages and of the different circles in which we moved.)

With a couple of dozen other young singers, I put on RAF uniform, and we sang national airs in front of a backcloth depicting Buckingham Palace. At the end, Buckingham Palace rose up into the air, revealing the seated figure of Britannia, which was the cue for 'Rule, Britannia' and tumultuous applause. By shuttling back and forth between Shepherd's Bush and Hammersmith in a motor coach, we were able to fit in five shows a day, and on one day six, because we went on to the Dominion, in Tottenham Court Road, and provided the finale for a *Midnight With the Stars* charity show. For a week's rehearsal and nineteen performances, I received four pounds ten shillings, less commission.

During the week, I heard that auditions were going on at the Lyric Theatre, Hammersmith, for a revival of the operetta, *Tantivy Towers*, by A. P. Herbert and Thomas Dunhill, so, between shows, I stuffed 'When a maiden takes your fancy' into my pocket and went along.

Still attired as an aircraftsman, I presented myself to Claude Powell, the musical director, who was wandering about the auditorium. He waved me up on to the stage, and I handed my music to the accompanist. Having sung the first verse of the aria, I saw in the dimness of the auditorium that Mr Powell had been approached by a colleague and was in consultation. I paused, momentarily, and the accompanist looked up and gestured to me to go on. I sang the second verse. I had never before got so far as this at an audition, and I was a little shaky on the words. Once again, I paused, and this time the gesture to continue came from Mr Powell, who was again giving me his attention. I launched into the third verse, which was virtually unknown territory. When I had stumbled through it, he gave me a cheerful smile and offered me a job in the chorus.

We started rehearsals the following Monday. This, I thought, was something of an achievement, to start an engagement immediately I had finished the preceding one. The principals were Maggie Teyte (later Dame Maggie Teyte), Steuart

Wilson (later Sir Steuart Wilson), Frank Phillips (afterwards to be one of the BBC's wartime team of news readers) and Dennis Arundell, whom I was appointed to understudy.

I discovered that the operetta had recently had an enormously successful amateur production in Guildford, and that had convinced the management that a professional production would echo its success: in fact, the lady who had directed at Guildford was to repeat that task now. The demands of the professional theatre are very different from those of amateurs, and there were raised eyebrows when she arranged for the guests at what was supposed to be a fairly wild Chelsea party to dance gaily round, hand-in-hand, like children playing ring-a-roses. Quite quickly, she was replaced by Dennis Arundell, who did what he could in the time, but even to my inexperienced eyes the production did not seem to get very far off the ground, and we expired after a run of two and a half weeks. The decision to close was taken suddenly, and the company was given only twenty-four hours notice. Legally, we were entitled to a week's salary, but although most of us needed the money, only two or three pressed for it, because the management were very nice people and we knew they had lost a great deal. Nowadays, the actors' trade union would not permit such consideration and sympathy, and I must say that we were a little piqued when we learned that all the orchestral musicians had been paid in full.

Among my fellow choristers were several people I knew from the Royal College of Music, and I shared a dressing-room with Frederick Sharp and Norman Menzies. Not only did we share a dressing-room, we also shared a dresser and this was a singular luxury. He was a Cockney youth named Joe, who brushed our clothes, cleaned our shoes, helped us off with our riding boots, and fetched us bottles of beer and eggs-on-chips from the café on the corner. Joe made life very much easier. I was to meet him again very soon.

After being pampered in such a fashion, my next engagement was a sad let-down – eight days on Devil's Island for a film called *King of the Damned*. Devil's Island had been built in a field near Northolt, and a very large crowd was needed for a sequence in which the prisoners revolted. To our indignation, on our arrival at the location we were given to wear a handful of evil-smelling rags that were fit only for the incinerator, and were led one-by-one behind a canvas screen to be made-up by a man with a spray gun, who squirted every square inch of us with orange-coloured stickiness. After the first day, I came equipped with my own rags and a bottle of body make-up.

The FAA and the agents were unable to provide a professional crowd of such dimensions, and casual labour was called in from all sources, including Salvation Army hostels and Rowton Houses. There were protests from professional crowd artists who found themselves in dressing tents next to verminous old men with sores on their bodies, and even angrier protests when clothes and personal possessions disappeared as soon as they were put down. After a while, a system of segregation was instituted.

They were miserable days. We sat in the dust of the compound under a hot sun while the sweat ran down our greasy make-up, and occasionally we got up to go through scenes of rioting and violence. In one scene, we were supposedly being bombed from the air, and we charged across the compound while mines exploded under our feet, blowing dirt and gravel into our faces and into every crevice of our bodies. Among my fellow convicts, I discovered my ex-dresser, Joe.

Although I had a reasonably presentable wardrobe, for some reason I had got on to the list for 'rough' crowds, and it was very seldom that I was picked for the easier and pleasanter scenes which involved standing about at parties or sitting in theatres. Occasionally, there would be mass auditions at the FAA, when casting directors would personally select artists from the assembled membership. This was a humiliating procedure, as we stood in line, in tails or dinner jacket or city suit, to be assessed like sides of beef.

There was an occasion when somebody telephoned me from Cricklewood Studios and asked me if I resembled an actor named Leslie Perrins. I bore no likeness to him at all, other than having a vaguely similar moustache some of the time, but I gathered from the tone of the man's voice that it could be to my advantage to say yes, so I did, adding brazenly that I had, on several occasions, been mistaken for Mr Perrins. I was then told that I must be at the studio early the next morning, and that I was to take with me a dinner jacket, tails, an opera hat, an evening overcoat, a dark blue double-breasted suit, a brown trilby hat, and a few other items. I gathered that the current production, which was called *Sunshine Ahead*, had over-run its schedule, Leslie Perrins had had to go to another job, and they needed someone to double for him in a few scenes which had still to be shot.

I was elated; this was certainly a cut above crowd work, and it would be valuable experience, as well as giving me an 'in' to a production company. In fact, I was so elated that I did not bring up the subject of money, which would have been an agent's first consideration. However, I did not worry unduly; the man on the telephone had sounded very friendly, and I was sure that the company would not be mean, especially as I was helping them to get out of a jam.

The next morning, I staggered to Cricklewood with two heavy suitcases. The director expressed disappointment at my lack of likeness to the absent Mr Perrins, told me to keep my back to the camera, and put me to work. In fact, I did one of the hardest day's work I can remember. Attired in my evening overcoat and opera hat, I assisted Eve Lister out of a taxi, paid the driver and escorted her to her front door; in my dinner jacket, I crouched behind some potted palms in what I took to be the foyer of a hotel, and watched some people come in; in my dark-blue suit and trilby hat, I climbed over a roof. . . . Always with my back to the camera, I was at it all day long.

When it was over, I repacked my bags and went to the cashier's office. He handed me a pound note and a shilling. I protested — I had finished the picture for them. . . Was that all my efforts were worth?

'Well, you didn't say nothing, did you?' he said. 'If you don't say nothing, it's crowd work, and you get a guinea.'

The Production Department at APS. Basil de Launay on the telephone, R.P, with a nice clear. desk, Denis Bullough and Ba On

Layout man, copywriter — and photographic model: as a blacksmith . . .

— and, with an artist named Pansy, as a baker's man. Some extensive retouching was needed

The Elmers Players present *Passing Brompton Road* at the Hillcroft Theatre, Surbiton. R.P. is on the left (*J. W. Debenham*)

My mother

My father

Sadly, I turned away. I had learned the valuable lesson that one must never be shy about discussing money – especially with a film company.

The most interesting of the films I worked on was Alexander Korda's *Things to Come*, from the story by H. G. Wells. The sequence in which I took part was set in the future. In the artificial sunlight of the clean, glass-walled city which had been built on the huge stage at Worton Hall Studio, Isleworth, some hundreds of young people, clad in the scanty white clothes which are all that would be necessary in a temperature-controlled climate, spent a carefree existence for some weeks. All was youth and light. There were many pretty girls and handsome boys chosen to appear in the foreground, and ballet dancers had been engaged to emphasise graceful movement. It was strange to come out at the end of a day into the gloom of a London autumn evening, and queue for a bus.

The exterior sequences, of the firing of the moon rocket, were shot on Dunstable Downs, and there was certainly no temperature-control there. Always in our flimsy garments, we froze.

In any mixed group, people gravitate towards others of the same age and the same background, and that was certainly true of crowd artists. In a very short time, I found myself a member of what we referred to as 'the gang'. We were all young, all stagestruck in one way or another, all from a middle-class background – and all broke.

Our social centre was a basement flat in Earl's Court inhabited by two dear and hospitable girls, Esme Easterbrook and Betty Farnan. The flat was large and almost devoid of furniture, because the two tenants had never saved enough money to buy any. When we had a party, which happened very frequently, each bringing food and drink according to his resources, we used to sleep on the floor to save money on fares home, because we would all be together again the next day. Esme was to have a long and rewarding career as a stage actress, but was to play in the West End of London on only one occasion; Betty was to die tragically young. The other members of the gang included a very handsome young man, Mark Innes-Kerr, who doubled as an all-in wrestler called Mark Milo; Johnny Esslemont, a Canadian who, as John Lemont, became a feature film director and was engaged to another gang member, Zita Dundas, who became a scriptwriter; Peggy Bloor, a buxom girl who played the accordion and occasionally appeared in variety; a singularly beautiful girl named Joan Bowles; Michael Moore, who was to have notable success in a long-running BBC radio comedy series called *Ignorance is Bliss*; an ebullient and intelligent young actor named Basil McGrail, who would surely have had a rewarding career if he had not been killed in the war; Alan Taylor, a rather earnest young man who had published a very long novel which none of us had read, and who had a girlfriend named Claire Marvin, who was a willowy model; and Bertram Tyrell, who went into pantomime every Christmas as one of the most lifelike cats ever to follow Dick Whittington.

Unexpectedly, I appeared in pantomime myself. It was at Wimbledon Theatre, which was very handy as it was only a few hundred yards from home. A friend named Erik Gifford-Stacey had been booked as a member of the pirates quartet in *Robinson Crusoe* and at the first rehearsal one of the members failed to turn up. Erik told the producer that he knew someone who lived just round the corner who was free, and he was despatched to fetch me.

'Can you sing tenor?' asked Erik when I opened the front door.

'Don't be an idiot, I'm a bass.'

'Never mind, you might get away with it. Come on over.'

I was interviewed in the Prompt Corner by Thomas J. Piggot, who was the general manager of the theatre. 'What have you done?' he asked. I mentioned the T. C. Fairbairn choir and *Tantivy Towers*, using the highest voice I could manage.

'And you're a tenor?'

'You could say I'm a sort of very light baritone,' I replied, not wanting to make a complete fool of myself if I were asked to sing a scale. Mr Piggot grunted a little doubtfully, but I was engaged.

One evening, some of us were released from rehearsal early and given eightpence each to go by underground to the West End to be fitted for our costumes at the premises of Chas. H. Fox Ltd.

'And get a move on,' said the stage manager, 'or they'll be shut before you get there.'

Obediently, we went out into the December darkness and started to walk the three-quarters of a mile to South Wimbledon Station.

There were five of us. In front were an elderly actor named Tom Squire and an Irishman who was not much younger named Liam Meagher: a few yards behind were Erik and I, with a portly actor in his late fifties, who wore a bowler hat and a black overcoat. His name was Cyril J. Rickards, and he had been engaged that day as a supernumary, to swell the ranks of the cannibals. We knew there would be a fuss if we did not get to Fox's in time, so we were walking fairly fast.

'You fellows are putting the pace on,' said Rickards to Erik and me. 'I've been told to take things easy. Heart, you know.'

We murmured sympathetically, but I am sure we did not slow down.

We bought our tickets and went down the escalator. A train was coming in as we reached the platform. Rickards was the last to board it, and as he came through the doors he went down on his knees and pitched forward. Erik and I thought he had stumbled, and turned back to help him to his feet, but he was limp and heavy, and saliva was bubbling at his lips. The four of us dragged him clear of the train and laid him on a platform seat.

'You two lads look after him,' said one of the elder members. 'We'll go on and get Fox's to stay open until you get there. Follow us as quickly as you can.' Tom and Liam got back into the train, which had been held up while the guard came to see what was the matter.

The train departed, and Erik and I, helplessly, tried to

revive our companion. One or two bystanders offered advice: 'Try to sit him up', 'Put his head between his knees', and various other impracticabilities. Then somebody said, 'I think he's dead'.

'Has anybody got a looking-glass?' I think that was my idea, because I had read somewhere that a mirror held to the lips showed if someone was still breathing. A woman produced a small looking-glass from her handbag. It did not mist over.

A porter appeared, and said he would telephone for an ambulance. It came very quickly, but it seemed an age. It was admirable how deft the ambulance men were at handling a stretcher on the steep slope of the escalator. It was my first encounter with death.

Fox's had kept open for us. That night I telephoned Raymond Mander to tell him there was a vacancy in the company for a supernumary. He applied for it the next morning, and got it. The show must go on, and a job is a job.

It was a good pantomime with a great deal of spectacle, including a first-rate storm scene, and it had a cast at least three times as big as would be economically possible today. Albert Whelan was Man Friday, and the Hengler Brothers, a brilliant pair of comedy acrobats, were the Captain and Mate. There were the usual superb idiocies in the script, as when Robinson, played by Sylvia Welling, was shipwrecked on the island and, walking onto the empty stage, said, 'Alone – on a desert island; but, never mind, love is everywhere.' Whereupon she sang a song called 'Love is Everywhere'.

We pirates had quite a busy evening; we sang sea shanties at various points during the first half, and then we blacked up and became cannibals for the early scenes in the second half, changing again to become gallant members of the rescue party for the closing sequence.

In one of the early scenes, to get an easy laugh, we sang 'The Ovaltineys Song', which was the theme of a Radio Luxembourg children's programme sponsored by the makers of Ovaltine. We had a bright idea that it might be possible to become sponsored ourselves, so I typed a letter to the manufacturers, telling them that we were singing the song twice daily to packed audiences and howls of delight, and what magnificent publicity it was for their excellent product, and we all signed it. 'They can't do less than send us a ten-pound tin,' we said to ourselves, 'and we can take it to a grocer's shop and sell it.' To our rage, all we had back was a letter offering a supply of songsheets to be distributed to the audience. I have tried to avoid drinking the stuff ever since.

Five of us shared a tiny box of a dressing-room under the stage, next to the band room, and there was a lot of acrimony because an Irish member never washed his feet and he stank the place out.

On the night of 20 January, which was my birthday, King George V died. We crowded into one of the chorus dressing rooms where there was a radio, and heard Stuart Hibbert reading the brief, repeated bulletin, 'The King's life is drawing peacefully to a close'. When the curtain came down, Raymond and I and one or two other members of the company went to join the crowds keeping vigil outside Buckingham Palace. As we walked down the Mall, we met people coming away. 'He's gone,' they told us. 'He's gone.'

A few days later, we paid our homage by waiting in a long queue and passing through Westminster Hall, where the King lay in state. An officer of the Brigade of Guards stood at each corner of the purple-draped coffin, his rifle reversed. As we went in, Raymond clutched my arm: the simplicity of the spectacle in that vast, historic space gave it an incredible theatrical quality.

Pantomime was followed by a dispiriting period of unemployment. I hung around the FAA, walked up and down agents' stairs, and tried to sell my freelance services as an advertising man. I managed to earn a few shillings painting a sign for a furrier in Balham, and as I surveyed my inaccurate lettering I wondered if he would accept it. Happily, he did. When morale began to sink to rock bottom I decided to do something decisive: if the managers did not want to hire me, then I would cut out the middle man and go directly to the public – I would seek out my own audience by singing in the streets.

I discussed the proposition with a girl named Kitty, whom I had met in *Drake of England*, and who supplemented her income from crowd work by playing the piano for the LCC on park bandstands. 'It's nothing to be ashamed of,' I assured her, 'we're just making a protest. We're performers, and we have a right to perform.' We decided that we could not risk busking in London, because there was always the likelihood of being seen by someone we knew: we must go out of town. I suggested Guildford, because it was prosperous and far enough away to be safe. We arranged to make our debut the following Saturday, when we assumed the town would be packed with happy, generous shoppers, glad to give a copper or two in exchange for musical entertainment. We conferred about a repertoire, and rehearsed 'Love in Bloom' and Tosselli's 'Serenade' as duets.

As a precaution, I looked in at Wimbledon police station and saw the desk sergeant. 'I wonder if you'll be kind enough to help me, Sergeant,' I said, in my breeziest juvenile lead manner. 'I'm writing a story about a man who decides to sing in the streets. Can you tell me what the regulations are? – would he have to get a license? – or does he apply for police permission? How does he set about it?'

'He makes sure he doesn't cause an obstruction,' said the sergeant, sourly. It seemed that my subterfuge was not deceiving him for an instance. 'If he does that, he's in trouble.' I thanked him and left. At least we did not have to fill out forms before we started.

We had decided to dress the part and wear old clothes. I think we both overdid it. When we met on Guildford station, I said, 'My God, Kitty, you look awful.' She thought I did, too. Before offering our wares to our public, we decided to have a final rehearsal and, as it were, get the feel of the hall, so we went into a backstreet where street musicians had probably never performed before. I don't think we would have won any prizes for our renditions, but at least they were as good as one was liable to hear in most streets.

We braced ourselves, and went to work in the High Street. The pavements were crowded. We walked in the gutter in single file: I went first, holding out a cotton bag which my mother had made for keeping counters in during her card party days. If you have been to Guildford, you will remember that the High Street is set on quite a steep hill. We sang 'Love in Bloom' going uphill on the left, and Tosselli's 'Serenade' coming down on the right. It was hurtful and wounding and almost insulting, the way people swept past, ignoring our performance. Nobody was taking the slightest notice of us.

Then I discovered the answer. Every trade has its secret and, quite by chance, I found the street singer's secret. It is not enough to amble along with a bag in your hand, you must thrust it under people's noses: it makes all the difference. In the next hour, we earned six shillings and eightpence, and this was at a time when the average working man's wage was about a shilling an hour. We looked at each other delightedly: if we could work as profitably as this, then unemployment was not a thing to fear.

But I lost my nerve! Coming along the pavement towards me was a man with whom I had been at King's. His name was Stoakley, and his father owned the *Wimbledon Boro' News*. Hastily, I turned my face away, and hoped that he would not recognise me. He did not – he did not even look at me – and perhaps it was not even Stoakley, but I wanted to call it a day. 'After all, we've learned how to do it,' I said to Kitty. 'We can do it any time now.' So we went to a restaurant and ate a good lunch, and then we went into a radio shop and asked if we could listen to John Snagge's commentary, because it happened to be the University Boat Race day, and we still showed a profit after deducting the cost of our meal and two Workman's Return tickets from London. We did not have to busk again, because some work turned up in the crowd in a Jessie Matthews picture, and the immediate anxiety was over.

One day, I was listening to a commercial radio station, and

I had an idea for a programme. Among the advertisers on Radio Normandy, among the laxatives and packet soups and soaps and gravy mixes, a firm was selling pianos, and pianos struck me as expensive items to be vended to a mass and mainly C-class audience. Furthermore, the programme was an unenterprising and conventional one of light music interspersed with spoken commercials, and it seemed to me that such a product called for special treatment.

Looking back at my idea, it still seems a good one. I proposed that a recording unit should travel the country, recording excerpts from the musical comedies and operettas in course of production by the principal amateur societies. This would stir up interest and excitement in each city or town visited, would flatter amateur performers, who were the most likely purchasers of pianos, by permitting them to hear themselves on the air, and it would enable dealers to tie in with window displays and local sales campaigns. In fact, everyone would benefit, including me, because I envisaged myself being hired to travel round with the recording unit and produce the programmes.

I had little idea how commercial radio worked, but I wrote a letter to the International Broadcasting Company, who were responsible for the English programmes from radio Normandy, asking if I might call to discuss an idea which could lead to our mutual profit. 'Profit' was obviously the right word to have used, because I was given an appointment to see the general manager, Richard L. Meyer.

The IBC offices at that time were in two or three houses knocked into one at the lower end of Hallam Street, on a site now covered by the extension to Broadcasting House. Mr Meyer kept me waiting for a quarter of an hour or so in a small anteroom littered with magazines and brochures concerning the commercial radio scene. I made good use of my time by noting down names and addresses for possible future use. From an enthusiastically written article in an advertising periodical, I learned that one of the brightest brains on the programme side belonged to a young man named Jack Hargreaves and there was a photograph showing him to be wide-eyed and keen, with a cigarette drooping from the corner of his mouth. Later, when I came to know Jack very well indeed, he was to confess that he had had a considerable hand in writing that article himself.

A brisk, small man, Richard Meyer listened to my idea, agreed that it was first-rate, and gave me two good reasons why such a series was not feasible: it was far too expensive, and there was no such mobile recording equipment available.

Having got that subject out of the way, we chatted for a few minutes, and my quick cramming in the anteroom enabled me to ask one or two reasonably knowledgeable questions. Mr Meyer told me of some of the difficulties in running Radio Normandy: for one thing, there was the problem of keeping a very small community of English announcers sober and happy in a rather gloomy fishing port in northern France. In fact, he said, yet another announcer had just quit, and did I know anyone who might be interested in the job? Indeed I did! What about me? I explained that I was an actor by vocation, knew quite a bit about advertising, was young, free and willing to travel. A few days later, I attended an audition at the company's recording studio in Kilburn High Road.

There were four of us awaiting our turns at the microphone: a young actor named Peter Bennett, who did not really want the job, because he thought he stood a good chance of getting a part in a new play at the Arts Theatre, a large man named Derek Faraday, who impressed us by letting it fall that he had appeared the previous evening in a BBC programme, and who was afterwards to run a successful recording studio himself; and a man who said he had been the Paris representative of *Punch* – and why *Punch* should have needed a Paris representative I have not to this day worked out.

When it came to my turn, I was greeted affably by Tom Ronald, who was later to be a senior BBC light entertainment producer. He took me into the studio, handed me a couple of commercials and a few announcements to read, and then disappeared through a door, presumably to listen elsewhere. When I had finished, he looked in again and said 'Thank you', and I said 'Thank you' and I went home. When I arrived there, a telephone message was awaiting me, asking why I had left, as they had wanted me to stay and make a test recording. I went back the next day and read the same pieces as before, making a disc which was presumably to be played to the powers-that-be. Some time afterwards, I was given the record and I still have it: on it, I sound very young and rather nervous, and my voice has affected, flat vowels.

I was then called to see Richard Meyer again, who offered me the job. I was to receive five pounds a week, but it would be paid in francs at an advantageous rate of exchange so that, in fact, it would be about six pounds ten shillings, and would I please leave for Fécamp, where the studios were, as soon as possible.

There was a rush round to obtain a passport and buy some new clothes. When I collected my travel ticket from the IBC office, it was a first-class one. I had never travelled first class before: at least, not with a first class ticket.

I was seen off at Victoria Station by my parents and by the entire gang, who showered me with confetti and good wishes, and despatched me with musical honours. I had the confetti-strewn compartment to myself, and the guard raised his eyebrows at the one ticket I presented for inspection and made several trips back along the corridor to see if he could catch my bride, whom apparently he presumed to be starting married life by travelling under the seat.

Dinner was served to me in the compartment, and a cabin had been booked for me on the boat. I had a couple of drinks in the saloon, and a turn round the deck with a chatty schoolmaster. I watched the lights of Brighton and Eastbourne grow smaller and fainter, and then drop into the darkness. It was 23 April 1936. I was now to be a broadcaster.

5

In the morning, while shaving, I looked out appreciatively across the quayside of Dieppe, where blue-trousered fishermen were clumping in and out of cafés, women in shawls were carrying long *baguettes* of freshly-baked bread, and small boys were scurrying to school, swinging satchels and dressed in short grey smocks. There was also that smell – that wonderful compound of Algerian tobacco, open drains, home-made furniture polish, coffee and aniseed – that powerful, all-pervading smell of France, which even topped the customary quayside smells of tar and oil and fish. I was the only passenger who had chosen to stay on board until eight o'clock, and a couple of resentful customs officers were hanging about just for me.

Having dumped my bags at the Gare Maritime, I went sightseeing, making a quick tour of the Eglise Saint Jacques, the fish market, the casino and the lawns, which reminded me of Hove. Then I bought a French film magazine, and breakfasted on coffee and croissants in a small café. I had not thought to look at a map to see how far along the coast Fécamp lay, but I had been told there was a bus service. I retrieved my luggage and hoisted it into a dusty, single-decked bus. Visualizing a bus ride of London dimensions, after the first twenty minutes I was sitting on the edge of the seat, ready to descend at a moment's notice. In fact, the journey took nearly two hours. We passed through straggling little towns and villages with such magical names as Veules-les-Roses, St Valery-en-

Caux, Veulettes-sur-Mer and St Pierre-en-Port. In each place we swirled to a halt in the square, and the driver hurled a bundle of newspapers to the ground before disembarking and embarking passengers, parcels, messages and livestock. I looked at the brightly-coloured cinema posters, some with familiar American names and faces, but most with French players unknown to me. As the crow flies, I was only 120 miles from home, but this was a new world.

At last we breasted a ridge of downland and looked down on Fécamp, a grey-roofed town set in a gap in the cliffs. There was a succession of harbours splitting the town in two, a magnificent abbey, a Gothic factory where Bénédictine is made and, on the cliffs on the further side, two towering radio masts. We descended the hill with a rush, charged across the harbour bridge, and took one final swirl on the gravel outside the Hotel de la Poste.

I dragged my suitcases into the glass-fronted bar of the hotel and bought myself a glass of white wine as a necessary preliminary to asking permission to leave my baggage while I went to the studio. Such was my ignorance that I assumed it would be in the same building as the transmitter. So I set off up a series of increasingly steep roads until I reached the masts, between which was a Norman-style building containing a large factory-like area housing what I took to be generators, tended by grey-coated technicians. I asked one of them to direct me to the English studio, and he pointed back down to the town, telling me I would find it in the Rue Georges-Cuvier.

I had been warned that the studio accommodation was not exactly the height of luxury, but I was a little shaken to discover that the English programmes were put out from a converted hayloft above what had been the stable of a private house belonging to a family named Legrand. I entered the insignificant building through a dark little ground floor office, in which two or three clerks were mailing circulars to members of the Association des Amis de Radio Normandie, and I was directed up some narrow stairs to the English domain. It consisted of a tiny office, in which there was barely room for a desk and a couple of chairs, a small workshop and our makeshift little studio. It was L-shaped and contained a six-turntable control desk for playing discs, a small table with a microphone mounted on it, and wooden racks, laden with records, lining the walls.

The morning transmission was over, and the only occupant of the studio was a grey-moustached military figure in his forties, who was putting away records. This was Tony Melrose, who had been empire-building in Africa before coming into broadcasting. He welcomed me and told me that John Sullivan, who was in charge of the English transmissions, was doubtless having a pre-lunch drink in the Café Thiers, and that he would telephone him to come and fetch me in the company's car.

John Sullivan proved to be a quiet, bespectacled person with a slight stoop and the manner of a benevolent public school housemaster. He was only 29 but seemed older. He was accompanied by his wife, Marie, a voluble, fresh-complexioned young woman with cropped fair hair. Disappointed in a love affair, Marie had come to France to forget, and had directed herself to Fécamp because, having listened to Radio Normandy programmes, she imagined there must be an English colony there. There was, but it consisted only of three or four browned-off announcers and a garage owner who acted as British consul. She had met and married John, and it is the only instance I have come across of a broadcaster marrying one of his fans.

John said he was sorry that the London office had not let him know exactly when I would be arriving: if he had known, he would have sent a taxi to Dieppe to meet me. I blinked. The idea of having a taxi sent forty miles to save me from the inconvenience of a bus ride opened up a scale of living completely unknown to me.

We went for drinks to the friendly Café Thiers in the main square, and then I was escorted to the Hotel Canchy et Chariot d'Or, the principal hotel in the town, where it was suggested that I stayed for a few days until I had made my plans. When

I murmured something about going to collect my bags, the idea was waved aside and I was told that the hotel porter would be sent for them. I then went into the dining-room and ate a solitary five-course luncheon. It was one of the best meals I had ever eaten, and if things continued to go like this I would have no cause to complain.

The room I was given was a large one looking onto a narrow side street where elderly women stood, selling fish from baskets. Their cries, which were unintelligible but evocative, were unceasing. So this is what Normandy fishwives sounded like! I even found it romantic. Above their heads was an advertising hoarding, and it featured a poster with which the whole of France seemed plastered at that time: apparently it advertised a product which cleared the nasal passages, and it depicted the head of a quite repulsive baby from whose left nostril flowed a stream of mucous which spelled out the brand name.

That afternoon I sat in the studio and watched the transmission. Running the control desk obviously called for considerable manual dexterity, but I thought I could probably acquire the knack, and so far as announcing was concerned I should be able to produce the amiable chat which was required. Certainly my knowledge of light music and of musical plays and films was as good as that of Tony Melrose and David Davies, the fair-haired young north-countryman who was sharing the afternoon transmission with him.

The Sullivans had invited me to dinner. They had rented the most modern house in Fécamp – or, to be accurate, the only modern house in Fécamp: among the redbrick, turreted nineteenth-century houses on the seafront, someone had planned and built a white bungalow on a raised site. Each of the two bedrooms had its own bathroom, and picture windows gave on to a patio facing the sea. The dinner was good, and the conversation was lively and pleasant. After the meal we settled round the radio with coffee and brandy to listen to a concert from London.

The next afternoon I was given a spell at the microphone, announcing records in a non-sponsored programme. I was nervous, but not unduly so, and I was happy to hear from my colleagues that the job had been done reasonably well. Part of the afternoon transmission consisted of an unrehearsed 'Children's Hour', based on the early BBC one, in which, for fifteen minutes, we read out birthdays, told stories and, when inspiration ran out, played discs. I was invited to take part as Uncle Roy. It seemed such a short time before that I had listened to the BBC's Uncle Rex reading out my own birthday.

Within a day or two, I was taking regular shifts as announcer or as controller. The transmission times were from eight o'clock until eleven in the morning, from half past three until six in the afternoon, and from midnight until one o'clock. On Sundays, which was the big day, we were on the air for an extra five hours. For all sponsored programmes, there had to be two of us on duty, one at the microphone and the other controlling the discs, but for non-sponsored (sustaining) programmes, or the late-night hour of dance music, one performed solo, using a microphone slung above the control desk.

As might be expected, there was some ill-feeling among the French at having the English programmes pumped at them, particularly in Fécamp itself, where the signal was so strong that it was difficult to tune in to other stations, so there was a rule that there must never be more than a minute and a half of talk between musical items. Of course, this put a stop to any form of dramatic programme or any extended talks, although the rule was sometimes broken in the case of comedy routines. Most of the time, we had a French announcer sitting in the studio with us, and every quarter of an hour or so he would interject a list of French titles for the next four or five musical items. The translations of the titles were provided by the Englishmen on duty and they were usually approximate and sometimes suggestive.

Some of the sponsored shows were fiendishly difficult to control. With all five turntables running (the sixth was kept for slow-speed discs only), a typical sequence would be: fade out the closing theme of a programme on turntable 1, open the microphone for the announcer to give a time signal, bang the time signal gong, cue the announcer to give station identification, fade in the signature tune of the next programme on turntable 2, crossfade to a pre-recorded announcement on turntable 3 and then crossfade to the first musical item in the new programme on turntable 4 — and it would all happen within fifteen seconds.

Before I was allowed on the air in a solo transmission, John said I must pass a test: while the studio was off the air, he gave me a script and a pile of records, and sat beside me while I did a dummy run. All went well until I was nearly at the end of the programme and then I put the needle down on a disc I had already played. I cursed, and imagined myself on the boat bound for England and more crowd work. But John grinned and said that everybody makes mistakes occasionally, and that he would pass me.

A few of the programmes were recorded on the soundtrack of ordinary 35 mm film, and were transmitted from a pair of soundheads which stood in the workshop. Sometimes French technicians would arrive to use them, because their programmes would occasionally include the complete soundtrack of a film which was showing locally. It seemed a curious form of radio entertainment, especially when, as sometimes happened, it was an American film dubbed into French, but I suppose it filled up air time cheaply.

In those days, the film used was nitrate stock, which was not merely inflammable but virtually explosive, but no safety regulations were observed. It was not unknown for someone to be seen winding back a reel with a lighted cigarette between his lips.

A transmission which presented a special kind of difficulty was the hour of dance music at midnight. The problem was how to be sure of staying awake until it was time to go to work. On any given evening, one or two of the English contingent would be out in the company's car, perhaps dining in Rouen or Le Havre, and others would be having an early night, which left the man on midnight duty to his own devices. After a heavy dinner and a few drinks, it was not a good idea to sit in one's room, for fear of dozing off, whereas to tour the cafés presented alcoholic dangers, and to go to the cinema meant having to leave before the main film finished. The only sensible approach was to make your dance music night your letter-writing night, and to sit in a café while doing it, drinking cup after cup of coffee.

The closing down ritual at the end of the midnight trans-mission was known as the 'Goodnight Melody'. It consisted of a wonderfully corny old disc by Ted Lewis and his Orchestra, over the instrumental section of which the announcer read some sentimental prose from the pen of Richard Meyer, based, I suspect, on an early New Year's Eve experiment by the BBC's J. C. Stobart called 'The Grand Goodnight'. 'And now the International Broadcasting Company's transmission is drawing to a close. . .' one read, while the sticky subtone of Ted Lewis's clarinet throbbed in the background. 'To those of you who are keeping watch on board the ships of the seven seas, fair winds and a good passage; to those of you who man the lightships on our sea-washed shores, may your night proceed peacefully, immune from fog. . .' You could not overact enough; it was fun to do. 'To bakers and newspaper workers . . . to young mothers, who tend their darling little ones . . . to those who are rising, to assure the early-morning shifts, may your day of toil be fruitful. . . .' I wish I could remember it all; there was a whole page of it, and I doubt if there is a copy in existence now. '. . . and to the rest of you, especially those who may be sick or suffering, Goodnight – and Happy Dreams.' It was enormously popular.

I settled down to the best training in broadcasting that it was possible to have. At the beginning of the day I pulled the switches and pushed in the plugs which put the studio on the air, I wrote scripts, ad-libbed countless hours of disc pro-grammes, worked at the control desk, made minor running repairs, and posted the log sheets at the end of the day.

I know it is a little late to apologize, but even now I feel guilty about the time signals we used to give. The clock above the control desk was not very reliable, and we were supposed to telephone the Paris observatory occasionally to put it right. That was a duty more honoured in the breach than in the observance, and the clock was often quite a bit out. Artistry came into it, too: it did not seem right to fade out the closing bars of a good piece of music in order to hit a raucous gong, so one was inclined to let the music finish before saying, with all the authority in the world, 'On the stroke of the gong, it will be ten o'clock precisely', and then hit the thing exactly on the beat of the finished tune. I hate to think of vessels having ended up on the Goodwin Sands because the master was ill-advisedly navigating on our time signals.

Because the IBC had had so much trouble in keeping their announcing staff – my predecessors had included Philip Hope Wallace, later to be a distinguished critic, and Alan Howland, who was to become one of the BBC's wartime newsreaders – they were making a real effort to ensure that we were reasonably happy in Fécamp. Apart from the company's car, which was at our disposal on a rota basis (although it was of limited use to me as I have never succeeded in becoming a competent driver), there was a week's paid leave in England every three months. Personally, my days in Fécamp were happy ones; I liked the food and the wine and the people, I enjoyed learning to speak French, and I was living very comfortably in the spare room in the Sullivans' house. On fine days I could swim, there were excursions to make, and there was a very attractive Belgian girl named Simonne to keep me company.

There was even an opera season – if you can call one opera a season. An operetta company played for a few weeks at the Casino theatre and, in the midst of *Phi-Phi* and *Rêve de Valse* and *No, No, Nanette*, they presented *Tosca*. I have seen better productions, and the stage lantern standing in a corner of Scarpia's study was obviously an oversight, but it was played with zest and enjoyment.

In July I had my first glimpse of Paris. Bob Danvers-Walker, who announced the IBC transmissions from Poste Parisien, was needed in London for a couple of weeks, and I was sent to replace him. David Davies drove me up, with Léo

Bailet, a bilingual girl from the south of France who did most of the Radio Normandy office work and occasionally obliged as a 'Children's Hour' Auntie. It happened to be 14 July in the year of the Front Populaire, and we arrived in the Avenue des Champs Elysées, where the studios were, to find rioting crowds, baton charges and bloodied heads. When we eventually edged our way through the crowds to the door of the building, we found it barricaded, and we had to make a furtive entrance through a door in a side street.

Poste Parisien, the smartest of the private stations operating in Paris, was very different indeed from Radio Normandy: the studios were modern, the equipment was superb, and there was a pleasant atmosphere of chic. We found Bob in the IBC office on the fifth floor, and he took me down to the studios to introduce me to some of the people with whom I would be working. Afterwards, David, Léo and I were his guests at the Russian nightclub, Scheherezade – or, to be accurate, we were the management's guests, because Bob's programme that night was a relay of the cabaret, a weekly job which I was to inherit for the next two weeks. Drinking the management's champagne in those luxurious surroundings, I reflected that it was the first genuine nightclub I had visited, and I was glad that I was visiting it in such happy circumstances. I fell in love with Paris at first sight, and the love affair continues still.

We left Scheherezade and returned to the Champs Elysées, where the political frenzy was still at its height. A market lorry pushed through the crowd piled high with round, severed objects, gleaming pallidly in the light of the street-lamps. The guillotine must indeed have been busy in the Place de la Révolution to have dealt with so many aristocrats in a single day. But of course those objects were only cauliflowers.

From Paris, I went to London for a couple of weeks leave. Esme and the gang gave a party for me, and, because one of the weeks was unpaid, I did a day's crowd work at Denham on a film called *Land Without Music*, with Richard Tauber, Jimmy Durante and June Clyde.

When I returned to Fécamp I did not go back to the Sullivans' villa but stayed for a month or two at the Hotel d'Angleterre, a holidaymakers' hotel on the front. It was kept by a portly widow, Madame Petel, who remains in my memory for refusing to admit me to the dining-room in shorts, and for selling John Sullivan some bottles of Johnny Walker whisky, which she had found in the cellar and which must have been there since before 1919, for the equivalent of three-and-six-pence a bottle.

Towards the end of the summer the hours of transmission were increased, which meant that more announcers were needed, and that meant more opportunities for social life. John Selby arrived, and then Robert Fellowes, who had been announcing at Radio Luxembourg and who was a nephew of the celebrated broadcaster, Christopher Stone. He was tall, thin and bespectacled, and a great man for starting a party, anywhere and at any time. At Cambridge he had been a climber, risking his life to place chamber pots on inappropriate pinnacles. He was amazingly surefooted; in Fécamp I knew him to run along the top of a wall in darkness, and swing his way, like a gibbon with his long arms and legs, across the front of the local brothel, knocking on windows and making remarks to the occupants which could only be described as provocative. David, Robert, John Selby and I moved to the Hotel Miramar, which was up on the cliffs to the west of the town. It was a rambling place with a four-room annex which we had to ourselves and where we could make all the noise we liked.

It was at the Miramar, one evening soon after we had moved in, that I walked through a glass door. I was alone in the hotel, my three colleagues being out on a party and the proprietor and his family out visiting friends. I had been writing letters in my room, and came downstairs to post them. As yet unfamiliar with the placing of the light switches, I groped my way down the dark staircase, and turned a corner into a passage, at the end of which I could see moonlight shining in the court-yard which separated the annex from the main building. I walked briskly along the passage, and straight through the door, which I had forgotten about. There was a moment of shock, a shattering of glass, and then an ugly spattering sound. I knew I had cut my face badly, and obviously my first thought was to get help. I crossed the courtyard to the back door of the main building. Inside, it was pitch dark and, once again, I could not find a light switch. Holding a squelching handkerchief to my face, I groped my way along the wall, through the kitchen and into the proprietor's living room, feeling for the wall telephone. I found it, and gave the number of the studio, where I knew that John Sullivan was working in the office. I asked him to send a taxi to take me to a doctor, and then groped my way back to my room, where there was light. There was a deep gash almost from the corner of my left eye, right down my nose. The scar is still a noticeable landmark on my rugged features.

John fetched me himself and took me to the surgery of Dr Maupas. With a strange sense of the macabre, he had decorated his waiting-room with brightly-coloured early nineteenth-century cartoons of primitive surgery, which must have been off-putting to other patients as well as to me. The doctor stitched me up, and I was driven back to the hotel with a thick dressing over my nose and left eye, held in place with a bandage round my head. It was my night to do the midnight dance music, but John kindly offered to do it for me.

To reach the town from the Miramar, one had to stumble down a steep cliff path which was not lighted. A night or two later, when I took over John's midnight transmission in return for his having taken over mine, it was starless and densely dark. I had my cliff-edge eye out of action and the field of vision of the other was narrowed to about 90° by the thick dressing. Having to turn one's head so far round in order to see to the side is liable to disturb the balance and at one point I wandered off the path and had to go down on my knees, in a fair state of fright, groping for the rough stones which marked the track.

That had been my second meeting with Doctor Maupas, who wore a moustache and an imperial beard and looked exactly like an illustration in an old-fashioned French primer. The first occasion had been when I had an attack of 'flu, for which he advised me to stay in bed on a diet of vegetable soup and champagne. This is a most effective treatment, and I have used it ever since: the soup gives you nourishment and the champagne keeps you cheerful.

For some time we had three Americans with us, Jack Savage and his Cowboys. Jack was a slow-speaking, hatchet-faced man who had been despatched to Europe to sell a product called Crazy Water Crystals, and his Cowboys were Bill Hite, a tall good-looking baritone singer, who also played the guitar, and Ted Grant, a small quiet violinist who had been with the Ted Weems Orchestra. They broadcast a fifteen-minute programme each day, with Jack doing the talking and the other two providing the music.

They had presumably taken a vow to drink dry the *département* of Seine-Inférieure, and they were setting about it in a dedicated manner. They were being paid lavishly, on an American scale, and the money slid out of their hands like quicksilver. There were only three or four taxis operating in Fécamp, and there was some resentment locally that one of them should be monopolized completely by the trio. Their driver, who was called Martin, took them everywhere, and participated in their revels.

There are many stories about the Cowboys, and one I am almost sure is true is of an occasion when, as they had not arrived at the studio a few minutes before they were due on the air, their hotel was telephoned and they were discovered to be still in bed. The faithful Martin was despatched to fetch them, and they arrived with only seconds to spare. Gummy-eyed, and hungover, they placed themselves before the microphone, still in pyjamas and dressing-gowns, and then looked at each other with hopeless shrugs: Bill had forgotten his guitar; Ted had forgotten his fiddle, and Jack had forgotten his teeth.

Robert Fellowes had known them at Radio Luxembourg, where they had stopped for a while before coming to Fécamp.

He recalled a time when Jack had disappeared for some days, being eventually found holed up in a country hotel moving about with his cupped hands held out in front of him. When asked why he was doing this, he replied that it was so that he could catch the little men if they should fall off their bubbles.

On hungover mornings, the tempo of their music grew slower and slower, and it was paradoxical to hear Jack advise his listeners, 'Watch your health, folks', when he was obviously suffering from severe alcohol poisoning himself. They were a talented act when they were at their best, and I became very fond of the western songs which formed their repertoire.

Later, when I had left the station, there was another resident cowboy act, Ed and Don, who were imported by the IBC from the United States. They were a great contrast to the Jack Savage group because they were quiet and well-behaved, and I often wondered whether the IBC had sent out a special call to the American agents, asking for teetotal cowboys.

An enthusiastic section of Radio Normandy's audience consisted of the crews of the ferry boats operating on the Newhaven-Dieppe route. One day we had a party of them over to visit the station. This led to our being looked after very well indeed on our crossings to and from England; in Dieppe, instead of complying with such boring formalities as customs inspection and passport control, we would join our maritime friends in the quayside Newhaven Bar, and be smuggled on board at the last minute via the crew gangway.

In November, we heard that Bob Danvers-Walker was leaving Poste Parisien to work permanently in London and that one of us would replace him. John Selby was the obvious choice, both from seniority (he had had a spell on the station before I arrived) and because of the excellence of his French. David was a non-starter because his interests were mainly technical, and Robert Fellowes was a newcomer. To my joy, Selby was offered an announcing job by the BBC, which he accepted, so I went to Paris.

There could have been few pleasanter jobs in the world. I

had to work quite hard on Sundays, but on weekdays I had only a half-hour evening transmission from half-past ten until eleven, of which one was the relay from Scheherezade, and Friday was a complete day off. Apart from an hour or two in the office every morning, attending to memos from London and getting out the discs needed for the evening transmission, the rest of the time was my own, with the whole of Paris to explore and play in. I also had a rise in salary.

In writing that the rest of the time was my own, I am forgetting one small and not particularly pleasant chore: it was an errand-boy job which had to be done two or three times a week.

There were a number of official bodies in the United Kingdom who wished to see commercial broadcasts in English from the Continent stopped: these bodies included the cabinet, the post office and the BBC, plus of course the press, which saw commercial radio as a competitor for advertising revenue. Because of this opposition, it had been difficult to arrange an efficient delivery service of records to Radio Normandy and Poste Parisien, which depended on a supply of the new commercially-issued discs, as well as recordings which had been specially made in the London studios. To send them to Fécamp or Paris by mail risked delay, possibly deliberate delay by an unfriendly postmaster-general; to send by rail and sea also risked delay (and do not forget that 78 rpm records were breakable!); to send by courier was expensive and did not obviate delay imposed by His Majesty's Customs – so a most ingenious, efficient and inexpensive system had been devised.

Just off the *grands boulevards*, there was a record factor's establishment, which supplied retailers with discs, not only those made in France but with those issued abroad as well. This meant that hundreds of boxes of records from all over the world arrived at their premises every week, so what could be simpler than to add a few more to the number? The records destined for Radio Normandy and for Poste Parisien were addressed to this firm – not so that the firm knew about it, of course, but so that one of the brown-overalled workers in the transit and packing department could intercept them and put them safely aside until they were collected by the Poste Parisien announcer. Naturally, for this service the man in brown overalls received a modest tax-free gratuity. I collected the boxes from him and readdressed them in a taxi on the way to the Gare St Lazare, from whence they were despatched to Fécamp. The whole Radio Normandy enterprise, with its vast turnover, was kept afloat by an occasional handful of francs pressed into the hand of a warehouse worker!

But then the story of prewar commercial radio was full of such madness. Little of its history has been written down, because the prejudice of the Newspaper Proprietors Association ensured that no mention of it ever appeared in the press, and the essentially popular nature of the programmes, plus the sudden collapse of the whole business soon after the outbreak of war, combined to deter any serious interest.

In the USA, right from the start – and the start of regular broadcasting was in East Pittsburg, Pennsylvania in 1920 – radio had been commercially sponsored, with the opening of new stations a virtual free-for-all. In such a small and densely-populated group of islands as ours anything equivalent to the American experience was obviously undesirable, so instant controls were brought into being, and those controls led to a monopoly which has endured until quite recently.

Representatives of 200 firms concerned with radio met in London in 1922, formed jointly the British Broadcasting Company, and obtained a licence from the postmaster-general to start a regular broadcasting service the following year. Rightly and properly, the standards set were of the highest, even if sometimes verging on the eccentric. The company's general manager was Mr J. C. W. Reith, a son of the Manse who held strict religious views and was intolerant of the slightest moral lapse: as a result, the programmes were very solemn on Sundays, with no light entertainment allowed. It was obvious that there was a great deal of money to be made by anyone able to provide a cheerful alternative to the BBC's 'Reith Sunday'.

In France the idea of commercial radio had blossomed

almost as soon as in the United States. The first regular French broadcasts were transmitted from a state-owned station on the Eiffel Tower in 1921, with a privately-owned station, Radio Paris, starting operations the following year. Both were transmitting commercial programmes, with Radio Paris quickly attracting the greater listenership because, as is usual with private stations everywhere, they were prepared to spend more money. In 1925, an enterprising young Englishman of Norwegian descent, Captain Leonard F. Plugge, scientist, inventor and ex-RNVR pilot, approached the management of the Eiffel Tower station with the idea that they should broadcast a talk on fashion in English, for which he obtained sponsorship from Selfridges. The feature brought in three letters from listeners. From the same station, Plugge himself broadcast a talk, 'Recent Developments in British Broadcasting'.

After this modest start, he set to work to acquire commercial radio interests in other parts of Europe. Travelling in his car, in which he had installed a radio (he claims to be the first man in the world to have had car radio) he began to search out concessions for transmission time, as well as founding a profitable secondary business by getting hold of the exclusive publishing rights for Great Britain of the programme schedules of continental stations, which he was usually given for virtually nothing in return for publicizing them. With the development and general use of powerful radio receivers, more and more people were regularly tuning-in to the Continent, and naturally they wanted to know what programmes were available. When newspapers and magazines bowed to the demand that they should publish such information they found that they had to go to Plugge for it – and pay. Probably his biggest customer was the BBC, which published a weekly magazine called *World Radio*.

In 1930 he formed the International Broadcasting Company, raising a capital of £100 from a man named A. E. Leonard. They took a one-room office at 11 Hallam Street, just behind the BBC's half-completed Broadcasting House, and their staff consisted of one junior typist. Their first broadcasting enterprise was a series of half-hour Sunday programmes from Radio Toulouse, sponsored by a record company, and those programmes produced the extraordinary number of 1,500 letters each week. Further transmissions were arranged from Radio Paris.

Next into the IBC net came Radio Fécamp, a sideline owned by Fernand Legrand, a junior director of the family firm that makes Bénédictine. He had begun radio transmission as a hobby, using a small hand-built transmitter which he kept behind the piano in his sitting-room. While chattering away on the air he mentioned, casually, the products of a shoemaker friend in Le Havre: the shoemaker was delighted at the unlooked-for publicity, and Legrand realized that there was a commercial future in his hobby.

One day, Leonard Plugge drove into Fécamp, on his way to a short holiday in Deauville, stopped at the Café des Colonnes in the Place Thiers, and began chatting to the proprietor. He was told about Fécamp's fishing industry and the Bénédictine factory, and also informed that the town would soon be celebrated on account of its radio station because the Legrand enterprise was expanding. Plugge abandoned his trip to Deauville, went to see Legrand, promised to provide bigger and better technical equipment, and proposed an agreement under which he could buy time for English programmes at the reasonable price of 200 francs per hour.

Transmissions in English began late in 1931, on a power of 500 watts, with an announcer named Max Staniforth in charge. Stephen Williams joined him at the beginning of 1932 and has told me that the only way up into the hayloft at that time was by means of a ladder, and that the single-record turntable was hand-wound.

Plugge did not find it easy to retail time on a small and completely unknown station. From his first sponsors he accepted goods instead of cash, taking radio receivers which were useful for listener research, and a supply of underwear for himself and his co-director.

As technical facilities improved, so did the business: the

name of the station was changed to the more impressive one of Radio Normandy, and the transmissions began to 'blanket the prosperous south', as the IBC publicity announced. In due course, as the transmitter power rose to 10 kws, not only could the station be heard in the south but also in the Midlands, although reception was poor in the north and in London. There was freak good reception in Iceland and, believe it or not, in New Zealand.

IBC transmissions were also heard from Radio Luxembourg, Radio Côte d'Azur, Radio Eireann and various stations in Spain, one of which broadcast only on shortwave. In all, experiments were made from over twenty stations, but most of the concessions arranged were for token transmissions of an hour or two each week, so as to have a foot in the door in case an opportunity came to expand, as happened in the case of Poste Parisien, which was transmitting in English for eighteen hours a week by the outbreak of war. One of the experimental outlets was in Ljubljana, Yugoslavia, where it was found that the inhabitants were devoted to the music of the bagpipes. (Could this have a connection with the descent of Celts into Bosnian territory in primitive times?)

Reports of the riches to be amassed led to cut-throat competition. Radio Luxembourg, owned and built by a French company, opened on 3 December 1933, its 200 kws making it the most powerful transmitter in Europe. A fierce legal battle was fought over the English concession, and at one time two rival teams of English announcers were in the Duchy, strictly forbidden to speak to each other. The winners of the battle, Wireless Publicity Ltd, still hold the concession today.

None of the stations putting out English programmes provided a news service. Not only would it have been an added expense but there was no call for it: because of an agreement with the newspaper proprietors, the BBC put out no news bulletins before six o'clock in the evening, and so listeners were not accustomed to hearing a lot of news. The desire for frequent news bulletins throughout the day arose, quite naturally, with the outbreak of war in 1939.

There was another reason why the concession holders were glad not to have to provide news: above all, they did not want to be accused of political bias, and it needs only a careless emphasis by an announcer to slant a news item politically. Politics were never mentioned in any context. When English programmes were restarted from Radio Toulouse in October 1937, there were shakings of heads because the Rt. Hon. Winston Churchill, MP, was included among the group of celebrated actors, musicians and sportsmen who were assembled for the opening transmission. In fact, Mr Churchill did no more than give a short address on 'The Peace of Europe', but his appearance was considered a dangerous precedent.

Religion, too, was almost totally ignored, although for a while Radio Normandy programmed a quarter-hour of sacred music early on Sunday mornings, with a short address by the Rev. James Wall, MA. So far as I know, no other station even acknowledged the existence of the Deity.

In the latter part of 1938, the IBC commissioned a firm of American radio research experts, Crossleys, to prepare a report on listening habits in London and the Home Counties. The survey produced some astonishing – and even alarming – figures. It showed that on Sunday mornings eighty-two per cent of the sets in use were tuned to commercial stations operating outside the United Kingdom. The opportunities for subtle propaganda of one sort or another, if anyone cared to take advantage of them, were surely serious – yet the BBC, under the control of Reith, appeared to ignore the situation. Even on weekday mornings, when the BBC was under no obligation to be solemn, the two main commercial stations, Luxembourg and Normandy, picked up sixty-four per cent of listeners. In the area surveyed, Radio Normandy had a larger listenership on weekdays, but Radio Luxembourg was slightly ahead on Sundays.

It is certain that Mr A. E. Leonard never regretted his £100 investment in the IBC because, at the end of the thirties, the company was showing a net profit of £100,000 per annum.

Captain Plugge had adopted a life-style to match: he lived

in a four-storied stone mansion in Hamilton Place, with a floodlit terrace overlooking Hyde Park. A household staff of fifteen ministered to him and his family, as well as looking after the dining-room with its fountains and its walls of pale green Carrara marble, the library, which was a Florentine room decorated in Renaissance style, the private cinema which seated fifty and – surely the most remarkable room in the house – the master's bathroom, which featured a dictaphone, a radio, four telephone lines and a television. His yacht, the *LennyAnn*, which was registered in Cannes, was reputed to have gold-plated taps. In the 1935 general election he had won, as a Conservative, the seat for the Chatham division of Rochester. Although he had hitherto pronounced his name 'Plooje', the temptation to use as his election slogan 'Plug in for Chatham' was so strong that thereafter he adopted the pronunciation 'Plug'.

While I was at Poste Parisien, Radio Normandy undertook to broadcast commentaries on a series of test-matches to be played in Australia. The BBC had announced that they were going on the air each morning at eight o'clock, which was the time when stumps would be drawn in Australia, to give a live résumé of the day's play, so the IBC decided to steal their thunder by starting a quarter of an hour earlier, at seven forty-five, with W. H. Ponsford's own commentary on the last fifteen minutes. Ponsford being a great Australian name in the world of cricket, listeners would naturally assume that the broadcasts would be coming direct from Australia (as were the BBC transmissions) although the IBC did not actually say that they were.

It was arranged that Ponsford, who was to cover the matches for an Australian newspaper, would send two cables to Paris during each day's play, the first timed to arrive at about 5.00 am, and the second at about 6.30. Bruce Anderson, a young Australian broadcaster who was on the IBC's London staff and who knew all about cricket, would be in Paris and would collect the first cable, taking it to the offices of the newspaper, *Paris-Soir*, where there was a small broadcasting studio on the top floor. There he would dictate a script to a typist, making up the details as he went along, describing the scene at the ground, which he could well imagine, and filling-out the bare facts in the cable. At 6.30 I would collect the second cable and take it to him, and he would continue dictating material based on this second dollop of information. Meanwhile I would read his script sheet by sheet as it came from the typewriter over the telephone to Charles Maxwell at Radio Luxembourg, because that station wanted to broadcast a commentary too. As neither Charles nor I had the least knowledge of, or interest in, cricket, it was a laborious procedure.

At 7.45, when Bruce's voice came on the air from Paris, going down the line to Fécamp, the notoriously poor quality of the French line made it indeed sound as if he were speaking from 13,000 miles away! Of course, one snag was that he did not know the current score, and he had to keep skating round that until, at eight o'clock, I was able to give it to him by taking it from the opening of the BBC transmission, which I received on a radio in the next room. It was an innocent deception, which doubtless gave pleasure to many – and it certainly kept the Radio Normandy listening figures up.

There was one incident which, although it caused some fuss at the time, could be looked back on with pleasure in the light of later events. One morning, Bruce arrived at the *Paris-Soir* building and found that he had forgotten his pass. The lift attendant, a surly, officious man with one arm, refused to let him in. Bruce, who spoke no French and had a lot of work to do, slung the liftman out of his own lift and took it up on his own. In June 1940, when the Germans occupied Paris, that liftman moved into the editor's chair. What better cover for a fifth columnist than to be the familiar, anonymous man who ran the lift, in whose presence nobody thought it necessary to be discreet.

Every Sunday evening, a special treat for me was to compere a forty-five-minute live broadcast by Willie Lewis and his Orchestra. During the late thirties, an absurd trade union ban prevented American musicians from playing in Britain and, as a result, Paris became the European centre for international jazz. Of a number of coloured bands there, Willie Lewis's was the most exciting. During the period when I worked with him, his players included such star performers as Bill Coleman, 'Big Boy' Goodie, Arthur Briggs, Herman Chitterson and Joe Turner. On two or three occasions, the BBC relayed the band in a series called 'Swing That Music' and, at Willie's request and by permission of the IBC, I was part of the package and thus made my first BBC broadcasts. At about the same time, I made my first appearance in radio drama, for Louis Merlin in one of his celebrated 'Madame Simone' programmes.

As the simplest way of living, I had taken a room in a *pension de famille* kept by an elderly widow in the Rue la Boëtie. It was a tiny room, which was all I needed, as I planned to spend very little time in it. It backed on to a courtyard where there was a good vegetarian restaurant – and it is the only one I have ever come across in France – and the headquarters of the Spanish Republican Party supporters, who put on frequent and noisy evenings of Spanish singing and dancing, ending with spirited renderings of *L'Internationale*. I did a lot of sight-seeing, and spent countless hours enjoying the sights, sounds and smells of the streets.

I went to the cinema a great deal. There was nothing of the senseless British system of releasing a film to dozens of cinemas at once and then letting it drop into oblivion; once a film was on the market it played in smaller and smaller cinemas at cheaper and cheaper prices until the prints were too scratched and tattered to be serviceable, so a look through *La Semaine de Paris*, or even a wander through the side streets off the *grands boulevards*, would unearth rare celluloid treasures. Many of the cinemas put on a late show, and I would often go after I finished my transmission at eleven o'clock. There was one in Montmartre which I sometimes visited after leaving Scheherezade, which showed a triple-feature at a knockdown price. Some of the American B pictures which had been cheaply dubbed into French were very amusing: the French dialogue seldom fitted the lip movements, which made the film virtually incomprehensible, and one sometimes came across a gem, such as when the sheriff was obviously saying to the heavy, 'Get out of town before sundown', while all that was heard on the soundtrack was *'Va t'en, salope'*.

Despite the usual financial problems, the French industry was reasonably prolific, with about 120 features being made every year. (The number being made in the United Kingdom was about 180, although that figure included many 'quota quickies'.) Many of them were independent productions, and the lack of front-office interference led to a freedom to experiment almost unknown in Hollywood and rarely known in Britain. It was the day of such adventurous directors as Marcel Carné, Jean Renoir, René Clair, Marcel L'Herbier, Jacques Feyder, Marc Allegret, Julien Duvivier, René Clément and Jean Gremillon, as well as some of the good Jewish directors expelled from Germany, and it was always a joy to watch Jean Gabin, Pierre Fresnay, Dalio, Harry Baur, Simone Simon, Edwige Feuillère, Louis Jouvet, Raimu, Michel Simon, Sacha Guitry and others among the incomparable assembly of players.

Of course, there was a great deal of rubbish as well, in the form of witless farces and foolish melodramas, but even those were good for one's French. An affection for French films has stayed with me through the years and, thanks to the National Film Theatre and the Institut Français, plus concentrated onslaughts on the cinema when I am across the Channel, I still manage to see about fifty in a good year.

My theatre-going was more restricted, because I had only one free evening a week. That also had to suffice for opera, ballet, music-hall and social engagements, but I remember Elvire Popesco and André Lefaur in Jacques Deval's *Tovarich*, and the Rip revues, as outstanding evenings.

6

When I had been in France for a year, I was invited to move back to London as a producer, so I found myself working in the Kilburn High Road studio where I had auditioned. It had been an Irish dance hall originally, and then it was the studio of the record company which issued the Sterno label. (In a very undistinguished catalogue, the only interesting Sterno disc I have come across is the first recording of 'Underneath the Arches' by Flanagan and Allen.) It was shabby and ramshackle, with a frayed grey carpet and hanging drapes round the walls which attracted every particle of dust. The control cubicle, which had no visual contact with the studio, was in an exterior lean-to. I shared a tiny office with Tom Ronald, who initiated me into the secrets of the producer's craft.

My immediate boss was Jack Hargreaves, about whom I had read such a glowing tribute while waiting for my first interview with Richard Meyer, and who had now joined the IBC. Jack's job was to devise a programme suitable for a sponsor's product, work with the producer to whom he allocated it for the first programme or two in the series, and then leave him to churn out the rest at the rate of three fifteen-minute programmes to a three-hour session. Sponsored programmes were a profitable sideline for artists, and many of the music hall and dance band celebrities of the day were in and out of the building. It was hard work and highly enjoyable. There were no union restrictions, and the producer worked his own control panel.

In July, I was entitled to a fortnight's holiday and of course I went to France. After a night in Fécamp, I moved on to Paris for a week. I had persuaded Simonne that the career opportunities in Fécamp were minimal and that if she were ambitious she should spread her wings and move to the capital. As she spoke Flemish, she had taken a job with the huge Dutch Philips concern at Suresnes, a riverside suburb. (The following year she was to move to Brussels, where she was killed in a road accident.) I spent my days lazing at a swimming pool and in the evenings when she had finished work, we visited the *Exposition*, which was in full swing. The acceleration of time as one grows older is a truism, but it is amazing to look in old diaries and see how much could be crammed into an evening. I suppose part of the reason was the ease of transport and the absence of crowds, but there was time to meet friends, have a leisurely dinner, do some sightseeing, and still get back to Suresnes at a reasonable hour.

For my second week, I went to Luxembourg to meet Robert Fellowes. It was the first time I had been through eastern France, and I was moved to see how many scars from the 1914–18 war were visible from the train. I checked in at the Hotel Kons and, as Robert was not due until the evening, I went to see an American film which was shown with French dialogue and German subtitles.

Robert was in his usual party mood, and he was accompanied by a friend, Ben Plunket, who was in the diplomatic service and currently posted to Washington. After dinner we went to a nightclub called Le Perroquet, where a charming girl named José mixed us something called a Depthcharge. (For those who like to live dangerously, the ingredients are equal measures of cognac, curaçao, cherry brandy, champagne and Kirsch; the whole disguised and made seemingly innocuous by the addition of ice and fresh fruit juices.) It was an orderly evening, but we got into minor trouble for being on the premises after permitted hours, and we found ourselves forming part of a group being taken to a police station to be fined, hemmed in by policemen who were wheeling bicycles. At one point, our encircling escort got into ragged formation, so we dived between two bicycles and ran down a side street. Very sensibly, nobody bothered to chase us.

The next morning, after a meeting with Charles Maxwell, the Radio Luxembourg announcer to whom I had dictated such reams of incomprehensible cricket material during the test-match transmissions, we crossed the Rhine and drove in Ben's gleaming Cadillac through the Moselle Valley, spending nights in Landau and in Friedrichshafen, where we visited a huge hangar where the Luftschiffen Zeppelin 130 was being built. Ill-advisedly, I took photographs despite a ban on doing so, although as picture postcards showing the monster dirigible in every stage of construction were on open sale, there did not seem much sense in the prohibition. In any case, it seemed unlikely that any future war would be fought in airships.

We drove eastwards to Oberammergau and spent a night by the gorgeous Dorf Walchensee, and then on to Munich, at one point driving through army manoeuvres and having a preview of some of the might of the Wehrmacht. In Munich, we surveyed the Brown House and the Temple of Honour and the other Nazi shrines, and took a rather childish delight in returning the greetings of 'Heil Hitler', with which every human contact was prefaced. Ben was notably more restrained about this than Robert and I: probably, because of his profession, he had a clearer idea of where it was all leading. We were all certainly impressed with Germany — with the efficiency, the smartness, the enthusiasm and the confidence of the people, or most of them — but there was a reserve and caution in dealing with foreigners which we found off-putting.

We were not impressed by the beer halls. We were in favour of drinking but it did not have to be so ceremonial, with all the clashing and clinking and toasting and waving of massive tankards, and we found the regalia and uniforms worn by middle-aged drinkers to be rather pathetic. I did not like the beer either; it was too heavy and sweet.

The following day we crossed into Austria and found a tremendous difference. At the exit post there were immaculate uniforms, polished boots, Nazi salutes, ruthless efficiency. It seemed that the Austrian guards, just a hundred yards further on, were taking a deliberate delight in providing a contrast, with casual friendliness, genial untidiness, unbuttoned collars, half-smoked cigarettes and cheerful grins.

In a Tyrolean inn, we struck what seemed a sensible solution to arguments about closing hours, and one which I would have liked to recommend to the Luxembourg police. We noticed that as midnight approached the attendance thinned out, and we were expecting a cry of whatever is the local equivalent of 'Time, gentlemen, please', but nobody bothered us. Some time later, a man came in, greeted the company politely and came round selling what we took to be raffle tickets. As they were only a schilling or two each and probably, we thought, in aid of some local charity, we bought some. An hour later, he came round again, but this time we explained that we would be moving on in the morning and would not be around when the draw took place. He became very persistent, and we then tumbled to the fact that it was not a question of raffle tickets but of paying on-the-spot fines for being in the place after hours.

I left my friends in Innsbruck and travelled back to Paris by a crowded night train. I saw Simonne, and said goodbye for what we thought would be quite a long time, and then took the evening boat train to Dieppe, having to stand all the way because it was Bank Holiday. I arrived home, very tired, at 6.45 on Tuesday morning. At seven o'clock, Richard Meyer telephoned and asked me how soon I could be in Paris. 'I can catch the nine o'clock from Victoria, via Folkestone-Boulogne,' I said. 'Why?' He told me that Jack Hargreaves was over there and had an idea for a series he wanted me to produce, and was that all right? I told him it was quite all right; there was a great deal of the *Exposition* I still wanted to see. All of a sudden, I was not tired any more. I was also thinking of the pleasure I would have in telephoning Simonne and saying, casually, 'By the way, I'm back in Paris.'

The series which Jack wanted me to produce consisted of cabaret programmes, for which I engaged Jeanne Aubert, Mabel Mercer, Una Mae Carlisle, Georges Seversky, and others of the great assembly of international artists who were in Paris during the summer of the *Exposition*. It was a very enjoyable seven weeks.

The *Exposition* – the International Exhibition of Arts and Crafts in Modern Life, to give its full title in English – was quite a production. Twenty thousand men had been put to work on a 250-acre site which extended from the Place de la Concorde to the Ile des Cygnes, a distance of over two miles and taking in parts of the river bank on both sides. The circumference was nearly five miles, and there were thirty-one gates. Forty-four nations co-operated and, considering the number of strikes, the organisers did very well to get as much ready for the opening day as they did.

Outside the main gate, at the Trocadéro, was a tower surrounded by the flags of the participating nations and this, according to the programme, was a monument to Peace. As soon as you got inside you saw no more optimistic nonsense of that sort, and observed the two massive opposing pavilions built by the Germans and the Russians, the German one topped by a massive eagle flapping its wings angrily at the two huge figures of a male and female worker, holding a hammer and sickle like weapons, which topped the Russian building. A little further on, the Spanish pavilion was celebrating peace by exhibiting Piccasso's vast painting of the bombing of Guernica.

The Trocadéro Palace had been rebuilt, rather well, to three times its former size, and below it were massive fountains, shooting jets of water towards a widened Pont d'Iena leading across to the Champ de Mars and the Eiffel Tower, the function of which, apart from exhibiting itself as a national monument, was to provide platforms for letting off fireworks.

The British pavilion was unanimously voted to be one of the

worst of the lot. It was small, and featured a layout for a weekend cottage, together with a lot of hunting, shooting and fishing gear, and a tasteful map of the British Isles on which the railway system was picked out in neon tubing. There was also a section on bookbinding.

Twenty-seven regions of France contributed pavilions, each built in a local style and, very wisely, concentrating on providing examples of local food and drink. The French colonies were also well represented, but mainly shoved away on the Ile de Cygnes which, by the driving of numberless piles, had been extended to four times its former size.

It was a magnificent playground, and all great fun if you ignored the propaganda and stuck to the more frivolous side. There was an enormous amusement park, and every day there were international sporting events, and a succession of foreign orchestras and ballet companies.

When darkness fell, the spectacle was magnificent. Twice a week, there was a gala of light and music, centred on the Trocadéro fountains, the river and the Eiffel Tower. There were eighteen different programmes, for each of which special music had been composed by such distinguished practitioners as Milhaud, Messiaen, Honegger and Ibert. It was an enchanting experience to take a seat in a launch that took you right into the middle of it all.

Among the scientific exhibits, I noticed a telephone which gave vision as well as sound. That was over forty years ago, and it still has not been commercially developed.

When I returned to London, the rough-and-ready days of Hallam Street and the Kilburn High Road were over. The IBC and its production division were installed in palatial offices and studios in a James Adam house in Portland Place – in fact, for a while I occupied an office with a ceiling painted by Angelica Kauffmann – and there was a charming mews pub, the Dover Castle, opposite the back door.

In those days, it was an unspoiled village pub in the heart of London: there were plain wooden benches and tables to sit at, and the bar stools were polished tree stumps from Windsor

Great Park. Tiny as it was, it was divided into a saloon bar and a public bar where drinks were a halfpenny cheaper and where pub games such as table skittles and dominoes were provided. The proprietors were a delightful old couple named Moyens. Mr Moyens, who was a small man, always wore a hat while on duty: in the winter it was a bowler, but on 1 May he changed it for the straw hat which he wore until 1 October.

Round the walls hung an extraordinary collection of old prints, photographs, press cuttings and curios, which had no common theme and seemed to have been accumulated haphazard. When we started entertaining our recording artists there, Mr Moyens observed that a few of our guests were coloured so, with a wise commercial sense, he decided to take down one of the more unusual items in his collection: it was a photograph of some long-ago lynching, with negroes hanging from the branches of a tree.

The rural atmosphere of the pub was heightened by the very frequent presence of Jos Angel, a burly red-faced man in breeches who ran the riding stables in the mews. His grooms, too, used the pub, cloth-capped men in shirtsleeves, often with straws in their mouths. With the ringing of hooves on the cobbles outside, the illusion of the countryside was complete.

The Moyens offered to provide a midday meal for us, and it was an excellent one. A generous cut from a joint with roast potatoes and a green vegetable was a shilling, and a substantial pudding was offered for threepence. For the greedy, an extra course in the form of a plate of digestive biscuits, butter and cheese was available for fourpence.

In France I had got in the habit of drinking red wine rather than beer or spirits, and I asked if it could be arranged for me to buy it in the bar, by the glass – which in those days was virtually unknown in an English pub. Nothing was too much trouble, and a vintage claret was made available at ninepence. We were well bestowed.

We spent so much time in the Dover Castle that Richard Meyer became worried. Was his production team a bunch of drunkards? Was some dreadful conspiracy going on? He sent his assistant, Frank Lamping, to investigate. After a few seemingly casual visits, Frank reported that the alcohol consumption seemed to be moderate, that nearly all the talk was shop talk, that we were bouncing ideas off each other all the time, and that the atmosphere was one of dedication and creativity.

Indeed, there was a corporate unity in that production division of a kind I had not encountered since I had been a member of a rowing eight, and which I have never encountered since. The dozen or so producers, writers and announcers who formed the creative nucleus ate, drank, laughed, moaned and clung together in a quite unprecedented way. Jack Hargreaves, Bruce Anderson, Tom Ronald, Aubrey Danvers-Walker, Dick Cartwright, Benjie McNabb, Edgar Blatt, Molly Gee, Wilfred Thomas and I, plus a few kindred spirits from whatever programmes we were dealing with, would spend our lunchtimes and evenings together in the Dover Castle, or move *en masse* to some party, theatre, nightclub or other social venue. Even on Saturdays, when we always worked in the morning, we rarely separated before the evening. On Sundays, unless there was work to do, or unless someone had organized an outing, we would stay in our respective homes and feel lost without each other. I suppose this huddling together was partly due to the fact that in a way we were outcasts, and there were no other people with whom we could share the same jokes. No matter how successful a programme was, it was never mentioned in print, and nobody, except a few close friends, would listen to our work critically: we were not in pure radio, as were the BBC people, and we were not in advertising, like the agency staffs who fed us work – we were on our own . . . we were pirates, and were proud of it. Perhaps it was part of our acceptance of independence that prompted us to adopt brightly-coloured and elaborately casual clothes, in contrast to the sober-suited men down the road at Broadcasting House.

The most memorable party we attended *en masse* was in Berkeley Square. The London County Council to its eternal shame and disgrace, was permitting the rape of this gracious seventeenth-century square. To start with, they had permitted the cutting back by forty feet of Robert Adam's fine 1765 frontage of Lansdowne House (now the Lansdowne Club) to permit a traffic flow to Curzon Street by the featureless Fitzmaurice Place: it then permitted the destruction of the lovely Georgian houses on the east side of the square, which were even older, so that, in their place, could be built the disgusting biscuit boxes of offices which now degrade the site.

The night before the houses were due to be handed over to the demolition men, the departing occupants gave a party. It was a party on a grand scale – because *everybody* was invited . . . the fact that you had heard about it meant that you were connected to the right grapevine, and the only other qualifications to be a guest were goodwill and at least one bottle. The houses were empty of all furniture, and holes had been knocked in the party walls so that one could stroll from one house to another. Nobody was counting, but there were hundreds of people, and joy was unconfined. I am sure that the ghosts of the Roaring Boys, Hellfire Club members, Regency rakes, Victorian Mashers and Edwardian Bloods must have looked on at the revels approvingly.

At the IBC we were joined, as musical director, by a plump Scot named Arthur Young, who became one of my closest friends. He was a brilliant pianist, composer and arranger, whose ideas were years ahead of his time. He played inventive jazz on two pianos with Reginald Forsythe, who was also a Scot, although a very dark-skinned one. Reggie was a dude, who spoke with strangulated good taste and a winsome lisp, and who was not at home outside the confines of Mayfair. Once when he and I were visiting Arthur, at a time when he had a flat in Knightsbridge, where the Berkeley Hotel now stands, Reggie got to his feet and announced that it was time he went back to the West End!

You could always tell the state of Arthur's finances, because he loved shiny things – shiny cars, shiny gold cigarette cases and lighters, and rings for his fingers. When he was flush, he had a complete set and then one by one, they would go.

He was completely improvident: when he had money he

spent it, when he hadn't he would move on until he found some: as a result, he never stayed in one place long enough to build a solid foundation. When he joined us, he had just returned from a spell in Berlin, where he had acquired a beautiful German wife, Katherine, who was a member of the Bechstein family (she was afterwards to achieve a certain amount of fame in Hollywood as Karen Verne), and they had an infant son, Alastair. Arthur, I knew, was earning £20 a week from the IBC, which was a good salary and more than twice as much as I was getting, but I also knew that some of that money had to go to a creditor who had caught up with him. With superb optimism, he took a delightful furnished house with panelled walls in Peel Street, bought a large, shiny American car, engaged a nanny to look after Alastair, and was to be seen, as was his wont, in the smartest places – oh, and there was a little matter of income tax. Fortunately, he never had to worry much about food and drink for himself, because his pockets were always stuffed with invitations: there was no-one in the world like him for making a party go.

He was aware when he accepted an invitation that he would be expected to go to the piano and give a performance which had considerable commercial worth, so he never had any compunction about taking a few friends with him. One evening in the Dover Castle he produced an invitation from his pocket and said, 'I have a feeling this should be a good party.'

'Who is giving it?' I asked.

'I don't know much about him, but he's very rich, and I'm told he has a fabulous house on the Terrace at Richmond. Let's all go.'

'All' was Arthur, myself, Molly Gee, an assistant producer who was a rumbustious character and a great party girl, and an aspiring actor named Tommy Duggan. We climbed into Arthur's car and set off for Richmond. It was late in the evening, and we had had a long, hard, hot day in the studio – we must have looked a scruffy lot as we stood in the porch of what indeed seemed to be a fabulous house.

The door was opened by a butler, who raised his eyebrows

in aggrieved surprise. Arthur flourished his invitation and we swept in. It really was not our sort of party. Drifting among potted palms and gilt mirrors were gentlemen in elegant tails and women in gorgeous gowns. Among the guests were a rajah and his entourage, and the purpose of the party was plainly to achieve some diplomatic liaison or form some trade pact.

Molly soon had a group of gentlemen around her, and was holding an enormous drink. 'What a bloody awful party,' she said, chattily. 'Whose is it?'

'Mine, as a matter of fact,' said one of the gentlemen, without enthusiasm.

Within a very few minutes Arthur was belting out his most infectious jazz at the piano, Molly was at her most outrageous, and Tommy Duggan was doing his unexpurgated impressions. Nobody was drifting about any more. The party began to take off, and it went on far into the night. Whether the diplomatic agreement was ever reached or the trade pact signed is doubtful, but I am certain that no guest present has forgotten the occasion.

On another evening I was alone with Arthur when he produced no fewer than three cards from his pocket. 'Not a very exciting lot this evening,' he said. 'They're small parties, and we'll have to take a bottle.' We bought a bottle of Scotch between us and went to the first one.

'Arthur!' cried the hostess delightedly, as she opened the door of her top flat in Earl's Court. No wonder she was so glad to see him, because she had somehow assembled a collection of dull people who were sitting around morosely, staring at each other. To be friendly, Arthur played a few numbers to try to cheer things up, but it was uphill work: after a while he shot me a glance which meant that it was time to be going. We told our sorrowing hostess that we had to move on to another engagement.

The second party was even worse, but the third was an excellent one and we stayed, so it was there that we handed over our bottle.

Arthur was a generous man: if he had two pounds in his

pocket, you were welcome to one of them — but if he had nothing in his pocket, then he was sadly unscrupulous. There was a celebrated story of a time early in his career when he had been in Berlin as a pianist with Jack Hylton's Orchestra. Needing money urgently, he had pretended to be in a position to arrange a concert appearance by the band, and had pocketed a sizeable sum given on account. He must have known that he would never get away with such a trick, but he lived for the moment and never thought of possible consequences. When Hylton discovered what had happened, he was livid with rage, paid back the deposit and sacked Arthur on the spot.

I had, of course, heard about this weakness and when, early in our friendship, he twice landed me with paying bills for the two of us on the flimsy excuse of a mislaid wallet, I had a quiet talk with him. 'Arthur,' I said, 'Not me — never again.' From then on, I trusted him implicitly, and he was as good as gold so far as I was concerned.

He was at the IBC rather less than a year before his next balloon went up and he had to disappear to France. In due course he reappeared, wearing dark glasses and with his overcoat collar turned up, to sound out the situation — but, as always, everyone was delighted to see this lovable man again, and even most of his creditors forgave him.

The facilities at our new recording studios were excellent, and we had two mobile recording vans, which meant that we could produce programmes before audiences in theatres and cinemas. An enterprising idea of Jack's was to record a music-hall programme at a large Kingston-upon-Thames cinema on Sunday afternoons. It was an elaborate and costly programme, and to make the public performances legal our audiences had to join a club, which was free to them, of course, as were the shows. Called 'Radio Parade', the programme was mounted without a sponsor and offers were invited for it. Within a few weeks, it was snapped up by Stork margarine.

After a while, to cut out all the club nonsense, it was moved from Sundays and inserted into the ordinary programme of films on a weekday evening. I took over the production, which meant that I would rehearse at Kingston in the morning, and then have the afternoon free to go on the river, sometimes taking some of the artists from the show with me.

Our mobility also lead to a plethora of cinema organ programmes, which were very popular. Some of these we would record at all-night sessions in suburban picture houses after the audience had gone home, or at early sessions before they arrived – and to listen to an organist playing 'Little Old Lady' or 'The Little Boy that Santa Claus Forgot' at 8.30 am in the Granada, Woodford, is only for those with strong stomachs.

As a promotion venture, a twice-nightly revue called *Radio Normandy Calling* was sent on tour round the music-halls, and I spent a couple of days with it each week. Joe Young, a Jewish comedian who had a wonderfully funny act called 'Buying a Theatre', ran an amateur talent contest during the first half of the week, and I turned up on Thursdays to judge the finals. The prize was a broadcast from Radio Normandy, and three or four of the winning contestants were included in a half-hour programme which we recorded on Friday evenings.

Ours was a harmless talent contest: there was no money prize and, above all, no offer of employment to the winners – just the fun and excitement of hearing themselves on the air (if they happened to live in an area where Radio Normandy could be received clearly, of course!) – but there were a number of talent shows on the road at that time which were doing a lot of harm. At every town we found youngsters hanging round the stage-door who had been 'discovered', had been offered five pounds a week to join a tour and to do so had thrown up safe jobs in factories or mills, starting off, they had hoped, on the road to stardom. After a few weeks, they had been sacked because better performers had been found or, in the case of girls, more amenable ones. They were now unemployed, but had not learned their lesson.

In addition to Joe Young, our bill included Alfredo and his Gypsy Orchestra, Maisie Weldon, the impressionist daughter of the music-hall veteran Harry Weldon, a pair of duettists called Ward and Draper, a dancing act and a line of girls. The world of the travelling music-hall has gone, and it was a strange world. Travelling fifty-two weeks in the year, if they were lucky enough to have 'a full book', the artists went from one set of professional digs to another. They got up late, breakfasted, called at the theatre to collect their letters, went to the pub until closing time, slept in the afternoon, went to the theatre in the evening for two performances, then back to the digs for supper and the exchange of 'pro' stories with other performers. They were vain, jealous, great raconteurs, and capable of consuming vast quantities of alcohol. Some of them did not vary their performances for decades. We tried to persuade Joe Young to learn a new act, but he had been performing 'Buying a Theatre' twice nightly for so many years that there was no hope of getting another script into his head.

Another personality trait that afflicted some music-hall performers, and an understandable one in view of their precarious calling, was that of financial closeness, and I well remember one instance. A Yorkshire comedian who was contracted to the IBC for a series of quarter-hour shows was offered a profitable pantomime engagement, and he asked if he might record in advance a supply of programmes to cover the weeks of his absence. The only feasible time to do this was at weekends, and I undertook to put six programmes in the bag for him one Sunday.

Starting at 10.30 am, I was still sitting in the control cubicle, with a production assistant named Lally Sprange and a recording engineer, at 7.00 pm, at which time our star said, 'Ee, Ah'me thirsty. Pub'll be open by now. Is there anyone about who'll fetch us some drinks?'

'I'm sure there is,' I replied over the talk-back, probably sounding cheerful for the first time that day. 'There'll be someone down at Reception. I'll 'phone down.'

There was a pageboy on duty, and I sent him into the studio. The comedian counted some money into his hand and, ignoring the thirsts of the three people who had toiled all day to make it possible for him to do his pantomime, despatched the boy to fetch *two* glasses of port, for himself and his wife.

One of the touring dates we played with *Radio Normandy Calling* was the Hippodrome, Norwich, and I decided to stay over until Sunday and visit my relatives at Holly House. There was neither a train nor a bus service to East Dereham on a Sunday so, after attending matins in the cathedral, I hired a bicycle.

It was pleasant to revisit the scene of my schoolboy holidays, and I enjoyed seeing Great-Uncle Jermyn again. By now, he was very old and living more than ever in the eighteenth century. He told me that, apart from cycling into Dereham occasionally to visit a bookseller friend, he seldom went out. I asked him if he ever went to the cinema.

'Oh, yes,' he replied, 'I did go once.'

'Only once?'

'That seems enough, really. I mean, I've seen it, I don't want to see it again.'

'What did you see?' I asked.

'Oh, it was a long time ago,' he went on. 'It was in a tent in the market place, and there was this man showing films. Very good they were. There was one of a dog running across some sands – I'll always remember that. You could see it quite clearly, you know – this dog running. Very good – but I don't want to go again.'

I tried to tell him that things had changed in the cinematographic world since his one encounter with it, but he was not really interested. After all, they got through the eighteenth century without films, didn't they?

The following summer, I spent three months touring the seaside resorts, recording concert parties and summer shows. I was delighted to find that many of them were using some of the same comic songs and sketches which I remembered from my childhood.

After a dummy run at Llandudno, I started my tour at Blackpool, recording Lawrence Wright's *On With the Show* on the North Pier. Internal air services were just getting going, and one of the new routes was from London to Blackpool. I suppose if you had a day to spare, it was a pleasant enough way to travel. I checked in at the Dorchester Hotel, where a limousine was waiting to take me, and others who had booked tickets for the flight, to Croydon. In due course, we took off for Liverpool, a flight of an hour and twenty-five minutes. At Speke airport, after a suitable wait, we changed into a smaller aircraft, but in the meantime someone had lost my luggage. We did eventually reach Blackpool, and so did my luggage, but I am sure it was quicker and far less trouble to take a train from Euston.

I had booked a room at the Metropole Hotel, which was the social centre for the Lawrence Wright organization, and I sought out the publicity man, whose name was Henry. He took me into the bar where Lawrence Wright, who under his pen name Horatio Nicholls had written many of the song hits of the past twenty years, was holding court.

At that time Mr Wright, a plump friendly man, was given to drowning whatever sorrows he had in drink, and he was not in his best form. Henry introduced me, and Mr Wright shook my hand as if I were the one man in the world he had always wanted to meet, and ordered drinks all round. I then went off to see the matinee.

Before dinner, I went into the bar again, and Henry again introduced me to Mr Wright, who again took my hand and again ordered drinks all round. 'You mustn't mind if I introduce you occasionally,' said Henry. 'Lawrie seldom remembers people, and it's the way the staff get free drinks.'

On With the Show was very good, and I think I still have the scars. The house was packed, and the only practicable place where a commentary position could be fixed for me was in the limes box, sitting on an iron grill. At the end of a two-and-a-half-hour performance, the pattern had impressed itself deeply into my person.

After the recording, Lawrence Wright gave a party in his suite for the stars of the show and for the IBC unit. He was now in a much better state and was remembering who people were. He rejected the resources of the hotel kitchens, and sent out for fourteen portions of that great local delicacy, tripe and onions. During the course of the party he developed an obvious attachment for Molly Gee, who was there as my production assistant.

Suddenly, he disappeared into his bedroom and came back wearing pyjamas and dressing gown, which his guests took as a hint that the party was over, and we all wished him good night. I was just getting into bed when I heard a gentle tap on my door. I had made no social arrangements to justify such a happening, so I called out 'Who's that?' There was no reply, but the sound of hurried footsteps beating a retreat. I looked out to see Lawrie running down the corridor, and remember noticing that for a stout man he had remarkably thin ankles. At breakfast, with a grin, Molly revealed that when he had asked her for the number of her room she had given him mine instead.

It was my first visit to Blackpool, and I enjoyed it. The golden mile had not yet been invaded by the property developers, and some of the side shows were still in tents. There was one which displayed a banner reading, 'SEE THE FORBIDDEN SEX RITES OF THE UBONGI WOMEN. ADULTS ONLY'. On a raised platform outside, a bearded man wearing a sola topee and a grubby white duck suit was expatiating on the strange and prurient things to be seen within, and indicating with a pointer the more interesting areas on some enlarged photographs of naked black girls. It seemed a promising shilling's worth so I paid up and went in.

Two or three dozen males were standing facing a small stage across which curtains were drawn. Exotic music blared from loudspeakers. From outside, we could hear the voice of the barker, telling passers-by not to miss their first and only chance to see the secret ceremonies. The tent became quite full.

At last, the music faded and the curtains parted. The crowd shuffled forward, eager for the first rite. But no, an elderly Indian appeared, bowed to us, and began to produce china eggs out of a cloth bag which he had shown to be empty. He then cut a piece of string in half and, magically, joined it.

This, we told ourselves, must be a preliminary act, put on while the Ubongi women prepared themselves. Then a girl appeared. A beautiful young Ubongi? No, she was white and plain, and dressed in a tattered gypsy costume: she carried a small table on which was a bowl of goldfish. After scratching herself, she went off, and the Indian made the goldfish disappear. The climax of the act came when, rather unconvincingly, he sawed the girl in half. When she had been put together again, the two performers took a bow, the man expressing the hope that we had all enjoyed the performance, that we would come again, and that we would tell our friends. The curtains were then drawn to, and we were shown out by a back door into an alley. Nobody said anything: we just looked at each other sheepishly and wandered off. We could hear the solatopeed man assembling another audience of suckers.

With the Blackpool broadcast we had something of a scoop because, between the time we recorded the show and the time it was due on the air, the theatre burned down and all the scenery and costumes were destroyed, an event which made front page news all over the country. But there, on Radio Normandy, were Bertini and his Band, and the Five Sherry Brothers and Tessie O'Shea, and all the rest of the big cast, still performing on a stage that no longer existed.

By then I had moved on to Scarborough and Worthing and other resorts. I was setting up several broadcasts at a time and, in addition, I had to be in whichever town 'Radio Normandy Calling' was playing in on Thursday and Friday evenings, so it meant travelling almost every day, and some of the cross-country train journeys, with their many changes, were very tiring. (I was delighted to discover a time-saving boat service which ran from Southend to Clacton. I wonder if it still survives.) Sometimes, a seaside recording could be fixed for a Saturday, which meant that I could travel in the recording truck with the technicians from the town in which we had been recording 'Radio Normandy Calling', but somehow all our trips by road seemed to take us over the Pennines at dawn.

I also had to make a trip to London each week to edit the

previous week's seaside recording and prepare a continuity script to be sent with the discs to the station. Another regular London task was to compere a series with the Welsh singer, Donald Peers. One way and another, my work was cut out, and it was galling to be greeted by my London colleagues with jibes about having spent the week lazing by the sea.

The seaside operation needed tact and guile; not only did I have to persuade artists to give us afternoon rehearsals when they would much rather have been relaxing on the beach, but I had to cajole directors and stage staff into revising running orders. Then there were unforeseen difficulties such as a threatened orchestral strike at Worthing, and the tiresome town fathers of Bexhill who let us get a whole programme ready before they decided that a broadcast sponsored by toothpaste manufacturers was not worthy of their municipal De La Warr Pavilion.

An additional chore was the intelligence network I was running. The BBC was broadcasting seaside shows too, and they were putting on the air some of the same companies which had been booked for Radio Normandy. Because our programmes were on disc, whereas theirs went out live, our transmission dates were more flexible and could be changed quickly when I got word of the BBC's schedules. On several occasions we were able to put a show on the air just a few days before it was broadcast by the BBC.

The shows I saw fell into four categories: first, the big, spectacular productions, such as those at Blackpool and Clacton, which had nothing particularly seaside about them and which could have succeeded on their merits anywhere; second, the medium-sized revues, which were liable to be tawdry and rather short on talent; third, the smaller troupes, such as the *Bouquets* companies, run by such seasoned 'pros' as Wilby Lunn and Reg Lever, and *Twinkle*, owned by Clarkson Rose, which worked in an up-dated Pierrot style. To my mind, this category provided the best all-round talent. (Clarkson Rose was a stern disciplinarian, and the first thing I saw when I entered the stage door of the Pier Pavilion, Eastbourne, was a notice on the board threatening instant dismissal to any member of the company appearing on stage displaying unsightly sunburn.) The fourth category, which mercifully was a small one, and of no interest for broadcasting, consisted of under-financed little enterprises occupying backstreet halls, where half a dozen people who would work for very little money capered about to an out-of-tune piano.

One thing which all the types of show had in common was a childlike approach to humour. Prewar holidaymakers liked the reassurance of the familiar: it was good to be able to nudge a companion as soon as a joke started, and say, 'Listen to this; it's a good one.' For the same reason, a comedian never put on a complete character costume or make-up when playing in a sketch: all he needed was a funny hat or a false nose, just like good old Uncle Fred did at home at the family Christmas party. It was a similar attitude to the holidaymakers of today who may go to Spain, but want the familiar comforts of English food and drink.

As it was difficult for me to plan far ahead, I seldom bothered to book a hotel room in advance, but took what I could find, being in an Imperial Palace one night and a Home From Home for Commercials the next. One evening, I arrived in Worthing, found a hotel on the front which could offer me a room and, as I was in a hurry to get to the Pier Pavilion, left my bag with the hall porter, telling him I would return later.

Having seen the performance and had a conference afterwards, it was about eleven-thirty by the time I got back. It was a wet night, with a gale blowing, and the hotel was in darkness, with the door locked. I knocked and rang for some time, before I was admitted by a very cross man who said, rudely, 'This hotel closes at eleven o'clock.' I told him how lucky he was to finish his work regularly at that hour, which was more than I could, and would it please be possible to have some sandwiches? 'Certainly not' was the reply. I sighed, picked up my suitcase from the porter's desk and made for the lift. 'The lift is not to be used after eleven o'clock,' barked the man. I changed direction and climbed the stairs to the third floor. My room was cheerless, and made even more so by the fact that the window was broken and the rain was beating on to the bed. I went downstairs again, and rang bells until the angry man reappeared, even angrier. I told him of the state of things upstairs, and asked if I might have another room. 'There's no other room,' he said, and I could hear the note of glee in his voice. I was too tired to trail round Worthing looking for another hotel, so resignedly I made again for the stairs, remembering all the small French hotels in which I had stayed and been assured of a civil reception no matter at what hour I returned. I could not resist a parting remark. 'This is a damned awful hotel,' I said, quite mildly. The man went white and began to quiver. 'I'm a religious man,' he said, 'and I cannot endure swearing.' With an effort, I restrained myself from demonstrating that I could swear very much better than that.

By the end of the tour, I was ready for my own seaside holiday. I went to St Malo, but at the end of a week I was summoned back to London to record a birthday show which was playing at the Granada Cinema, Tooting, and which we were to broadcast as a precursor to a new series of 'Radio Parade' programmes, each of which would be recorded in a different Granada. It was the biggest stage broadcast I had ever tackled: it had an enormous cast, including a large orchestra, a Guards band, several star comedians, some first-rate singers, a chorus and a fan-dancer. The fan dancer presented a problem, until I had the inspiration of persuading 'Monsewer' Eddie Gray to give a running commentary. He was brilliant.

With a complete lack of interest in politics and world affairs I had been ignoring all talk of imminent war, but now it was no longer possible to do so: in fact, on Wednesday, 28 September 1938, it looked as if the die was cast and nothing could stop the conflagration. On that day, I was rehearsing for an appearance as the back legs of a comedy horse. I was back in the Granada, Tooting. This edition of 'Radio Parade' was to be a Wild West one, in which a comedy horse had been added for some visual fun, and as I felt I wanted to have as wide and varied an experience of show business as possible, I had volunteered to play the back legs.

The morning rehearsal was a very unfunny occasion. Both David Miller, who was producing, and Bobby Howell, who was conducting his orchestra, had served in the 1914–18 war, and were sickened at the idea of the whole useless beastliness starting again. In an atmosphere of deep gloom and intense anxiety, the company muddled through the show. We then broke, to let the audience in for the afternoon films.

At about 4.15 the news came through that Mr Neville Chamberlain was to fly again to Germany to try to make Hitler see reason. In a flash the tension lifted. There was hope again. Chamberlain had worked magic on his previous visits; he would do it again.

It was a cheerful cast which reassembled on the stage that evening for the recording. Euphoria had set in. It certainly had for our compere, a Canadian variety artist named Ted Andrews, who was seen to be reeling happily about the place and obviously in no state to face a microphone.

I looked round for David Miller, but he was not there. Come to that, neither was our announcer, Bob Danvers-Walker. I could hear the closing scenes of the feature picture which was unrolling on the screen between us and the audience. There was not much time – it had to be Plomley to the rescue.

I climbed out of the horse skin and sent my compliments to the driver of the recording truck: would he kindly take my place? It was obvious that I would have to go on in place of Ted Andrews, although I had never read the script and his part was a long one, including some comedy sketches: it also looked as if I would have to do the announcing, which involved reading the commercials, and apparently I was to be the producer as well. I was going to be busy.

First of all, somebody had to tell Ted Andrews he was not to go on, and that was something I was not looking forward to. Luckily for me, two white, breathless and shaking figures arrived at the double – David Miller and Bob Danvers-

Walker. They gasped out that they had been to Walthamstow Granada, where the previous week's programme had been recorded, by mistake. It did not seem a very likely story, as they had been rehearsing all the morning at Tooting, but there was no time to argue, and they do say that euphoria can take odd shapes.

I put on the cowboy jacket and ten-gallon hat which had been ordered for Ted – neither of them fitted, but then this was supposed to be a comedy show – and, as Bob Danvers-Walker finished his opening announcement, I walked on. I could manage a western accent, and I got through the sketches, which were fairly predictable, with reasonable success – but I had to be careful of such stage directions as 'He draws a gun', because nobody had thought to give me one.

The show went on – after a fashion – and the general feeling of national rejoicing was such that authority, in the person of Richard Meyer who was sitting in the audience, turned a blind eye.

I spent most of the winter shuttling back and forth across the Channel as, in addition to the various series on which I was working in London, I was given eighteen more cabaret programmes to produce in Paris. These were more elaborate than those of the previous winter, and the artists I engaged included Lucienne Boyer, Jean Sablon, Josephine Baker, Pils et Tabet, Léo Marjane, Garland Wilson and the Quintet of the Hot Club of France, with Stephane Grappelli and the incredible gypsy guitarist, Django Reinhardt. Like every field of activity, broadcasting is cursed with a certain amount of paper work, and I had to give Django a form to sign – I think it was an authorization to broadcast an unpublished number of his – but I had to read it out to him and indicate where he was to put his mark, as reading and writing were two accomplishments which he had never bothered to master.

Garland Wilson, a slim, elegant negro pianist with huge eyes and wide flared nostrils, had come to Europe as accompanist to Nina Mae McKinney in 1932 and was to stay until the war started. He was playing at Le Ruban Bleu, an upstairs room above Le Boeuf sur le Toit, where piano jazz was a feature. Born in West Virginia, he had learned his job in gin mills, 'where they gave you a piano with eighty-eight keys and expected you to use every one of them'. He had a fine sense of humour but a rackety life-style: when he had finished his night's work, towards dawn, he would go 'cruising'. His social life would continue until quite late in the morning, and then he would go to bed.

I fixed our recording session as late in the day as possible, at about four o'clock, and told him that I would collect him from his Montmartre hotel. It took quite a long time, but eventually I got him out of the hotel and across the road to a café, where I gave him a drink to get the juices flowing again.

We went by taxi to Poste Parisien, where I had booked the main studio. I told him to sit down at the piano and loosen up, and went into the control cubicle to apologize to the engineer for being late. When I went back into the studio, it was empty. I thought perhaps he had felt he needed another drink and had gone downstairs to the Café George V. After a few minutes, I went down to look: he wasn't there. I explored the Poste Parisien loo and again drew a blank. Precious minutes of our recording time were ticking away: where was he?

Then I noticed that one of the wall drapes was moving very slightly, and there were certainly no draughts in that studio. I went over and pulled the drape back. Lying on top of a radiator cover which could not have been more than seven inches wide was Garland, cosy and warm, and fast asleep.

Once again I woke him up, pushed him over to the piano and got him started on his first number, a fast tempo version of 'Alexander's Ragtime Band'. He did not think the first take was good enough, but after that he played like an angel.

An important musical event in Paris that winter was the visit by Duke Ellington and his Orchestra. Because of the trade union ruling I have already mentioned, they could not visit London, so hordes of jazz-loving Britons crossed the Channel. Naturally, I had booked seats for the first of the two concerts at the Palais de Chaillot, and took a girlfriend. Afterwards, we went to the Dôme, which was then at the height of its popularity, and sat on the covered *terrasse*. Among the crowds milling in and out were composers, songwriters and arrangers from London, all with scores under their arms which they hoped to have a chance to show to the Duke. Snippets of news were being passed around – 'He's gone out to eat, but he'll be at the Swing Club at about two o'clock', or 'He's going to Chez Florence', or 'He'll be at Bricktop's'.

Having nothing to sell, I had no interest in joining in the pursuit and, after a while, we went for a quiet drink at La Cloche, a small nightclub run by the songwriter Jean Delettre, at which he gave a chance to unknown young singers. It was also frequented by composers, who officiated at the piano in order to obtain a hearing for their new songs. (On one occasion, I had dared to get up and sing there myself, accompanied by none other than Alex Siniavine.) The club was having a poor night, and when we went into the dimly-lit room we saw that only one table was occupied. That was Jean Delettre's own table, where he was entertaining three guests. I whispered to my companion that one drink there would be enough, and then we would go and find somewhere a little more cheerful.

As our eyes grew accustomed to the semi-darkness, I saw that one of Jean's guests was a dark girl called Sugar, who was the friend of Henry Starr, of the coloured duettists, Browning and Starr. She looked across and waved, and we waved back, and she called across, 'Why don't you two come on over?' so we crossed the dancefloor and greeted her, and said hello to Jean, and then Sugar indicated the other two people at the table and said, 'Do you know Irving Mills? – and this is Duke Ellington.'

There followed several hours of sheer delight, as we coaxed Ellington into talking about his music and about his band. Then Irving Mills, his manager, went off to bed, and Jean went to cash up – not that there was much in the till that night – and the remaining four of us went to an all-night restaurant in Montmartre. The place was packed, but nobody recognised The Duke. At about five o'clock, he said he would have an early night, so we put him into a taxi. One of the last things he said to me was, 'I'm a hell of a bad pianist; I wish I could get better.'

The next morning, I met Arthur Young, who had been one of those in and out of the Dôme with a score under his arm. 'He disappeared,' said Arthur. 'He didn't show up at the Swing Club, and he wasn't at Bricktop's — nobody knows where he got to.' With studied casualness, I supplied the information.

A new tour of *Radio Normandy Calling* went on the road, with an entirely different cast. Topping the bill was a dancing act quite useless for broadcasting but very good for the box-office, Edna Squire-Brown and her Glamour Girls. Miss Squire-Brown was what would be called nowadays a stripper, although that seems a rather vulgar word for such a well-brought-up young lady. She was beautiful, elegant, and had an upper-class manner that betokened Cheltenham Ladies College or Roedean. Every week, she was visited at the theatre by her father, who was an aristocratic-looking gentleman with white hair and perfect manners.

Her act was refined. One part of it was a fan dance, but the fans were large and her handling of them deft, so that the audience did not benefit by so much as a glimpse of bosom. The climax was the moment when, on a certain beat in the music, she flung out her arms — and the fans — to each side, but at the same instant a switch was pulled and there was a complete blackout. It was all so fast, so unexpected and so smoothly executed that nobody was sure if he had seen a flash of her nude body or not. Then, during the blackout, which lasted several seconds, she turned and ran up a flight of steps behind her and, when the lights came up again, she was posed at the top, with her fans again strategically placed and her Glamour Girls attractively grouped around her.

The production was being inexpensively mounted, and there was a minimum of rehearsal, with the artists meeting on the stage of Margate Hippodrome on Sunday afternoon and putting the whole show together in time for the first house on Monday evening. As I was again to be responsible for a weekly broadcast from the show, I sat in at the rehearsals, which were directed by a well-known touring manager named Leon Pollock.

All was going well at the first performance, which I watched from the front stalls, until the climax of the fan dance. Miss Squire-Brown flung aside the fans, and the blackout was exactly on cue – but instead of it being held for several seconds the lights came up again almost immediately – and no naked lady looks her best when viewed from below and behind while she is going up steep steps. When the curtain came down, she was the angriest lady I have ever seen.

Commercial programmes continued to get better. In the IBC studios, or those of other production units, Sir Thomas Beecham conducted the London Symphony Orchestra in popular classics (his sponsor, naturally, being Beecham's Pills), and Louis Levy and his Gaumont-British Symphony played film music; Arthur Askey and Richard Murdoch continued the inspired clowning they had begun together in the BBC's 'Band Waggon'; Vic Oliver, Bebe Daniels, Ben Lyon, Tommy Handley, Gracie Fields, George Formby and the Western Brothers all signed long-term contracts, and the dance bands of Carroll Gibbons, Jack Jackson, Harry Roy, Lew Stone, Roy Fox and Marius B. Winter provided both sweet music and swing. I still possess recordings of a few of the programmes. Even by present-day standards they make good listening. The pace may be slower, but they have an overall atmosphere of good humour and relaxation, and they sound reassuring – and then, as now, radio could do a good job at reassuring.

In the summer of 1939, my responsibilities included producing the 'Stork Radio Parade' (which had again changed its format and now featured Peter Yorke and his Orchestra and some excellent singers and guest artists), compering the Donald Peers series, which went on and on, and recording programmes in provincial music halls by Reginald Foort at his mammoth touring organ.

The latter enterprise was a splendid and slightly dotty one. Reggie Foort had been voted by the readers of the *Daily Express* as the most popular radio artist of any kind, and he was big business. His managers had commissioned a specially-designed five-manual theatre organ to be made in America by the Moller company; it came neatly into sections to be transported about the country in five huge pantechnicons. It weighed twenty tons, which meant that the stage of some music-halls had to be shored-up, and as the swell-box was forty-two feet wide and deep in proportion, it occupied almost the full area: as a result, all Reggie's supporting acts had to be frontcloth artists. For the finale of the show, the whole front of the organ was flown up into the flies, and the audience saw the immense assembly of 2,000 pipes glittering in the lights, while Reggie opened up everything and shook the whole building with a thunderous version of 'Land of Hope and Glory'. There were many hazards, of course, especially in bad weather and, on more than one occasion, only four-fifths of the organ arrived in time for the first house on Monday evening.

Our recording sessions were held during the day before an invited audience. Our sponsors were a firm of toothpaste manufacturers and the tickets were distributed by the shops which stocked their products. It was at a session in a Midland town that I encountered a rather worrying incident.

While I had been at Fécamp, my first listeners' mail had reached me, and I acquired my first steady fan, Bubbles. She wrote on very expensive stationery in rather middle-aged hand-writing, and sometimes she wrote as many as three long letters a day, full of passionate declarations of love and sealed with silver wax. Every tune I announced was taken as a personal message to her. 'When you said "The Thrill is Gone", my heart sank, as I thought all must be over between us,' was the sort of thing she would write. 'I had noticed a cooling off in your voice ever since you announced "Goody, Goody" yester-day – but then you followed it with "The Glory of Love" and my spirits lifted again.'

This one-sided correspondence had continued ever since, varying in intensity from a deluge of letters to a gap of several months during which I heard nothing. Part of her fantasy was that we had an infant son, and she would chide me for not going to see him more often. Sometimes she would communicate by telegram which, even then, was quite expensive, especially to the Continent. At Christmas came a briefcase or a silk evening scarf, which I had not the heart to send back, but acknowledged in carefully-worded formal notes. Sometimes she enclosed an engraved visiting card which revealed her real name – but she always signed herself 'Bubbles'.

It was during the rehearsals for that Reginald Foort session that I suddenly realized that I was in Bubbles's home town. I thought no more about it until just before the recording was due to start, when the stage-door keeper brought me one of her cards with the message that she was waiting to see me. What should I do? Acting on instinct, I asked him to say that I was very busy (which was true) and unable to see anyone. In a few moments, he came back with another message: Could she please have a ticket for the show?

I panicked. Suppose she should make a scene! Suppose her strange infatuation should turn to hate when she saw its object in the flesh! Suppose she had a gun! 'Please tell her that you haven't been able to find me,' I said to the stage door keeper, 'and that there are no tickets left.'

After the performance, I heard that she was still waiting. My caution persisted: I went out through the stagedoor in the company of two technicians who were about the same height and the same age as myself, and we all had our overcoat collars up. I had a glimpse of a middle-aged lady in a bright green hat; she was heavily made-up, with scarlet lips in a dead-white face. Curiously, she did not refer to this near-encounter in any subsequent letter.

Details of the matter were afterwards put to a psychiatrist of some eminence, with the question, was my caution justified? His verdict was that in the circumstances my actions had been exceedingly sensible.

The postal love affair came to a sudden end about six years later, after a thoughtless line I wrote in a script for a BBC series called 'To Town on Two Pianos'. It featured Arthur

Young and Reginald Forsythe on two pianos, with Stephane Grappelli playing the violin and Elisabeth Welch singing, and each week I recounted the fictitious adventures of the two pianists, whom I characterized as layabouts whose favourite haunt was a sleazy Soho drinking club. Obviously, the club had to have a name, and one day I said, unthinkingly, 'I know, let's call it Bubbles's Club,' thinking that the name evoked fairly accurately one of the afternoon clubs which flourished at that time and which were frequently run by, and named after, a faded ex-chorus-girl who was nominally the proprietor. I must have unwittingly offended poor Bubbles, because I never heard from her again.

When the war started, there were many reasons why Reggie's organ tour had to be abandoned, and the instrument was sold to the BBC, who gave it a fixed home in a disused chapel in South London. When they no longer found it useful, it was sold to a cinema in Holland and, when last heard of, it had returned to the land of its birth and was a great attraction in a pizza parlour in San Diego.

All in all, I was a very happy young man. I had been promised a temporary secondment in the USA which, to a radio man, was the promised land. There was talk of war on the front pages, but it was easy to skip the front pages and turn to the show news. Surely there could never be a war – the whole idea was too childish.

7

On Saturday 12 August 1939 I set off with a girlfriend for a fortnight's holiday in the south of France. I badly needed a holiday; I had taken no time off for a year, and had been working much too hard. Recently, I had found myself waking in the night clicking imaginary stopwatches.

We spent a night in Paris and took the early train to Marseilles. It was a first trip south for both of us, and we were fascinated to watch the countryside change; to see grey slates give way to pink tiles, to see the vast acreage of the Burgundy vineyards, and travel alongside the fast-flowing, ever-broadening Rhone. At Marseilles, we marched down the steps outside the St Charles station and booked in at the vast, impersonal Hotel Terminus. The evening we spent in exploring the *vieux port* and sitting on a café terrace, watching the parade of variegated humanity. In those days a multiracial society was a novelty.

The next day we moved along the coast to Ste Maxime, where we stopped for a week or more. Despite a determination to ignore the international situation, the headlines announcing the German and Russian alliance could not be other than alarming, and when we moved further east to Cannes we found mobilization orders posted, and there were impressive musters of fierce-looking African troops who were, so rumour said, to be let loose in the mountains against Mussolini's forces.

On Thursday evening we decided that, in a spirit of bravado

Crowd artist. Listening to Hans Söhnker sing in a film called *Faithful* *(Warner Bros.)*

Clive Brook comes to the rescue of Madeleine Carroll in *The Dictator*. R.P. looks suitably villainous in the bottom right-hand corner *(Toeplitz)*

There was not much going on in Fécamp

The control desk in the English studio at
Radio Normandy

Young broadcaster *(Frank Buckingham)*

and as a last highlight of our holiday, we would take a trip into Italy; so, early next morning, we began a tour of the coach agencies. At the first two or three we were told that all excursions across the frontier had been cancelled, but then we found a kiosk in front of which was parked an open motorcoach with 'SAN REMO' chalked on the windscreen. We bought tickets, and gradually the coach filled up. After half an hour's wait in the hot sun, we set off along the Grande Corniche.

Just before we reached Mentone, our driver, who looked like Harold Lloyd, stopped the coach and made a speech about the dangers of going into Italy: he said that, instead, he would take us on a drive through some picturesque areas of the French Alps. My companion and I and a man in the seat across the aisle protested: we said we had paid to go to San Remo and that we insisted on going there. We turned to the other passengers and demanded their support. So did the driver. None of them responded to either appeal, but sat still with placid, expressionless faces. Eventually, a young man leaned over to me and said, in English, 'What's the row about?' It then dawned on us that all the other occupants of the coach were either British or American tourists, who had not understood what was going on. My French-speaking neighbour across the aisle (who turned out to be an Armenian lawyer with an American passport) and I then did some spirited rabble-rousing, and we soon had all our fellow passengers on our side. We were going to San Remo, we said, even if we had to push the coach there ourselves.

Harold Lloyd shrugged his shoulders, said gloomily that it would serve us right if we found ourselves interned before the day was out, and let in the clutch. At the frontier post at Ponte San Luigi, we were welcomed most hospitably by the Italian guards, although our passports were checked carefully, and one of them confiscated an out-of-date *Evening Standard* which I was carrying. Nothing we saw in Italy seemed in the least warlike. On the way back, my girlfriend slept all the way through the frontier formalities, and the guard who inspected our coach gallantly gestured to me not to wake her.

We left the coach at Monte Carlo, to go to lose the traditional few francs at the casino, and then returned to Cannes for an end-of-holiday celebration supper.

We were up at 4.30 to catch the autorail to Marseilles, but it was running late and we missed our Paris connection. The station was in chaos: all the porters had been called up, and in those days it was not the custom to travel light. The trains were *declassés*, and very crowded. It was dark by the time we arrived in Paris and we found the city blacked-out, but in an inefficient and half-hearted manner. We had a depressed drink outside the Café George V on the Avenue des Champs Elysées, which had been my 'local' in Poste Parisien days.

If the journey from the south had been a trial, it was a picnic compared with the cross-Channel trip the next day, and we only got aboard the train at the Gare du Nord by falsely claiming to be members of a conducted tour. All over Europe, everyone was making for home.

At the studios, I found an atmosphere of alarm and despondency. Most of the senior members of the staff had been issued with uniform overalls, lanyards, whistles, knives and axes, and the building was littered with ladders, buckets and sandbags. So far as the IBC was concerned, the war seemed to have started.

All the overalls had already been distributed, but I was given a map and the title of Area Staff Marshal, or some such, and told that I would be responsible for picking my way among the ruins of that part of southwest London centred on Wimbledon to carry instructions to staff members living in that area. It was the generally held opinion that savage air attacks would be unleashed by both sides immediately war was declared, and that within a few hours London, Paris, Berlin and a number of other cities would be devastated.

We had a practice air raid drill, set off by a klaxon. There was a great deal of whistle-blowing and running about by all the chaps who had overalls, and the rest of us were herded into a shelter in the basement. A record player had been installed, presumably to drown the explosions, and somebody put on a dance tune called 'And the Angels Sing', which produced slightly hysterical laughter. All recording sessions scheduled for the week had been cancelled, as the sponsors had decided that there would be no profit in stockpiling programmes for listeners who were probably about to be incinerated.

On Friday, which was 1 September, Tom Ronald came into the producers' room in mid-morning and said he had been told that the Germans had invaded Poland. We switched on a radio and heard the BBC confirming the news, and telling us that their own emergency plans were going into operation, with broadcasting confined to one channel. It was also announced that Britain was to be blacked-out. That evening, I went to the Holborn Empire, where Reginald Foort was playing his touring organ, and where I should have been recording him. There were about half a dozen people in the audience.

The next afternoon, I walked across Wimbledon Common to Putney. Children were being assembled for evacuation to the country, householders were criss-crossing strips of paper across their windows as an optimistic precaution against blast, and ARP posts were manned. At the little Globe Cinema, a French film was being shown, and I went in to see it. It was Jean Renoir's *La Grande Illusion*, one of the most powerful pacifist films ever made, and it had a numbing impact. I went back to Wimbledon in a completely blacked-out District Line train which stopped at darkened stations, but which station one was at, or even if one was at a station at all, was sheer guesswork. Later, a lighting system giving a subdued glimmer was supplied in public transport, but to start with there was nothing.

On Sunday morning, soon after eleven o'clock, I was lying on my bed, reading. My parents called upstairs to say that the Prime Minister was on the air, and I switched on to hear the words '. . . this country is now at war with Germany'. A few minutes later, the air raid sirens wailed. It was the first time we had heard that eerie sound, which picked up from district to district, no two sirens starting or stopping together, and it sent a fearful foreboding to the pit of the stomach. Mother,

163

Father and I gathered in the little hallway on the first floor, where we would be screened from flying glass. To give myself a feeling of doing something useful, I collected some gardening tools with a vague idea, based on ARP announcements which I had not bothered to read properly, that they might be useful in dealing with incendiary bombs. We decided that if there should be bombing nearby, we would retreat to a cupboard under the stairs. After about half an hour, the all-clear sounded, and Father insisted that Mother took a draught of sal volatile to calm her nerves, although she seemed quite cool and collected.

Now that the country was at war, it was time to clarify to myself my own attitude. I felt angry and aloof. I told myself that I was a pacifist and an internationalist, and that I had no personal quarrel with the Germans or with anyone else. In any case, I maintained, war solves no problems but creates a thousand new ones, and is as pointless as quarrelling neighbours throwing rocks at each other's houses. The whole bloody business was to be an intolerable intrusion in all our lives; it could go on for years, and millions of people could be killed or maimed, including myself and those dear to me. In short, I wanted no part in any war.

My views were selfish and ingenuous, but that was how I felt. I explained my attitude to my father, who had been deeply upset at the sight of tearful evacuee children being herded into trains and buses. He disagreed with me, and we had our first, and only, quarrel. I reminded him that German children were also being evacuated, and were just as pathetic and tearful.

There were bulletins on the radio every hour or two, and I listened to them all, because there was always the tiny hope that national leaders would come to their senses and call the whole thing off. I even got up at four o'clock in the morning to hear the first bulletin of the day, but there was no news of any significance. At the studios everybody turned up for work as usual. My only function as an Area Staff Marshal was to call on a telephoneless office boy in Tooting, who seemed to have got his instructions wrong.

It was obvious that under conditions of wartime security, Radio Normandy, a frivolous commercial station broadcasting from a foreign country, could no longer operate as before; in fact, it was already off the air. The IBC management had hoped that on the outbreak of war they would be able to turn over the recording studios and the entire excellently-trained staff, as a going concern, to the War Office for forces entertainment or some other official use, but there were no takers. An elaborate promotional book called *This is the IBC* had been put into production for circulation to advertising people, but when war became certain the order to print had been cancelled: it was now decided to go ahead and spend the money, so that copies could be distributed in Whitehall. However, the book did no good.

The production staff were invited to hang about on half pay to see what, if anything, happened, and the technicians set up a laboratory in the basement to experiment with time fuses and various lethal devices. One ingenious idea they worked on was a propaganda shell. Visualizing a trench war on the 1914–18 pattern, with a relatively narrow No Man's Land between the opposing sides, they devised an unbreakable loudspeaker with a spring-loaded spike on the end, which could be launched from a mortar in our trenches, land on its spike and then, by means of a trailing cable, subject the unfortunate Hun to a deluge of propaganda.

A prototype was made, and a party from the War Office, which included the foreign correspondent and broadcaster Vernon Bartlett, came to a demonstration. I was one of those on the roof of 37 Portland Place deputed to send the thing earthwards at a given signal, whereupon it would land in a flower bed and serenade the visitors with a record of 'Don't worry 'bout me, I'll get along' followed by a speech about the possibilities of the idea delivered by Bob Danvers-Walker. I don't know how impressed the War Office dignitaries were, but as soon as they had gone the technicians rushed the device down to their workshop, where they found that the loudspeaker magnets had been shattered into a myriad pieces, and nobody could fathom how the cone had been able to work in the gap.

In the absence of an official takeover, the management decided that a logical step would be to try to get the station back on the air and use it to broadcast programmes in English for the entertainment of the British Expeditionary Force in France. Radio Normandy's fine new transmitter at Louvetot, which had been in use since June 1938, had been requisitioned by the French government and absorbed into the national network, but the old transmitter at Fécamp, which was still in good working order, was not in use.

With Plugge busy among his political friends in London, another IBC director, George Shanks, was working wonders in Paris. Shanks was the company's *éminence grise*: a tall, languid man of great charm, he had been a fellow-pilot of Plugge's during the First War. Of Anglo-French descent, he had spent much of his childhood in Czarist St Petersburg, and was blessed with a satisfactory financial background stemming from a celebrated champagne firm. Among a number of orders and decorations which had been bestowed on him was the richly-named papal one of Privy Chamberlain of Sword and Cape. His contacts were many and most useful.

In London, a committee of British notables was formed, under the chairmanship of Field-Marshal Lord Birdwood: in France, approval and co-operation was obtained from the Ministère des Affaires Etrangères and the Haut Commissariat à la Propagande – or certain sections of them. (The fact that the station could be heard better in southern England than in northern France seemed irrelevant, as did the fact that relatively few British troops in France were likely to have access to the cumbersome radio receivers of the thirties pattern.)

The station was to be rechristened Radio International, although a little anxiety was expressed in some quarters about the unfortunate similarity to the title of the communist anthem, 'The Internationale'. The broadcasting day would start at 7.00 am with cheerful British light fare which would continue non-stop until 8.oo pm, when there would be a pause in transmission long enough for the carrier wave to die down. Then a Czech unit would take over, broadcasting propaganda and calling itself the Czech Freedom Station. After a couple of hours of that, the carrier wave procedure would be gone through again, and then an Austrian unit would go on the air until midnight as the Austrian Freedom Station.

We all leapt into activity again, which was welcome after an aimless existence of writing revue sketches which would never be performed, playing endless games of darts, and organizing concerts for Civil Defence units which, like us, had nothing to do.

The studios were to be back in Fécamp (when the Louvetot transmitter had opened, they had been moved to Caudebec, on the Seine) and they were to be manned by the existing Radio Normandy staff, augmented by Bob Danvers-Walker, Philip Slessor and Charles Maxwell, who would go out from London. The teams of Czech and Austrian broadcasters would be recruited in Paris.

Programme schedules were speedily put together, and Radio International was soon on the air. The salesmen had been at work, and a number of Radio Normandy's pre-hostilities sponsors agreed to have their old programmes rebroadcast. Obviously, the lengthy commercials which had originally formed part of the programmes were no longer suitable, because 200 words of chatty patter about how to make a delicious supper dish for your husband with wonderful, instant Boxo hardly fitted the image of the new audience, but there could be no objection to the simple statement that, 'The next half-hour is sent to the British Expeditionary Force in France with the good wishes of Boxo, the sauce that does you proud.' It was decreed that the word 'sponsorship' was never to be mentioned: our advertisers were to 'participate'. Commercial radio was on the air again!

The new station quickly picked up most of Radio Normandy's listeners, who were delighted to hear the familiar voices and the familiar programmes, and doubtless doubly delighted to hear them without the commercials. Furthermore, the station was on the air for many more hours a day than Radio Normandy had ever been.

Not so delighted was Fernand Legrand, who had begun it all by starting Radio Fécamp and now had his transmitter requisitioned by the government and handed over to the IBC for nothing. 'Participation' was a fine new word, but he was one person who was not participating. During the first days of transmission, before a direct line was arranged to Civil Defence headquarters in Paris, the station had to stop broadcasting every time the local siren sounded. As that siren was on the roof of the Bénédictine factory it was said that it was sounded much more frequently than was necessary.

Another section of the community not at all delighted was the Allied High Command. To ensure that hostile aircraft did not use radio transmissions as navigational aids, it was decreed that all transmitters should be synchronized, which meant that each station had to broadcast from two or more transmitters on precisely the same wavelength. Radio International was probably the only station in any belligerent country not to be synchronized. Protests were made both to the French and British governments, with demands to have the offending station silenced, but as nobody in authority knew exactly whose baby Radio International was, nothing was done.

George Shanks was alerted about these protests so, in association with his French contacts, he bought the beautiful seventeenth-century Château d'Epone at Mantes, thirty-seven miles down the Seine from Paris, where a new transmitter would be built and paired with the Fécamp one. Technical equipment was at a premium, because the French government needed all it could get for propaganda purposes, particularly in Africa, but it was on such difficulties that Shanks thrived.

Two or three weeks after the station opened, reports reached London that Philip Slessor was very unhappy in Fécamp. On one occasion he had hurled his headphones across the studio, and he was said to be showing all the signs of an approaching nervous breakdown. It was put to me that, as future plans included the production of live programmes at the station, it would be useful to have an announcer there who was also a producer, and would I replace Philip? Now that the programmes had settled down to a steady weekly routine, there was little for me to do in London, so I agreed.

I crossed the Channel on the night of 11 November. From Victoria, I had a blacked-out compartment of the train to myself, and I sang all the way to Newhaven, to cheer myself up. I was further cheered by being asked for my autograph by a customs officer who had been a dedicated listener to Radio Normandy. Nobody on board had thought to take down depressing framed photographs showing the damage done by the enemy to the same ship during the 1914–18 war.

The Fécamp studios were new, but all the faces were familiar. George Busby was managing the station, and his secretary was Beryl Muir, whom I had known in Paris. The announcers, apart from the arrivals from London already mentioned, were David Davies, Ralph Hurcombe, Maurice Griffith and Godfrey Holloway. There was plenty of work to do, mostly ad-lib disc-jockey work, hour after hour of it, but because of wartime security, every word that was said had to be written down. That meant that every time you announced a disc you had to write down, while the disc was playing, every word you had said, which didn't give you much time to think of something bright to say about the next one. Of course, that way of working was not strictly in accordance with the rules: our scripts should have been written in advance.

One day, George Busby came back in a panic from the weekly meeting he attended in Paris with George Shanks and his political friends at the Ministère des Affaires Etrangères: somebody had asked if all scripts were being officially censored. Indignantly, George had replied that of course they were – so, to be on the safe side, we had some rubber stamps made and spent many hours stamping all the pages of scribble covering every announcement made since the station opened with 'Visé. Ministère des Affaires Etrangères' and initialling each one. It was my one and only experience of being a censor.

169

We put out frequent news bulletins, compiled by Beryl Muir from a Havas Agency teleprinter. Beryl's English, as befits a Scots girl, is perfect, but she had lived so long in France that she had developed one or two idiosyncrasies which showed up in her bulletins. One of them was her translation of *canons* as cannons, and there was an echo of days long past when one found oneself reading at the microphone such phrases as 'There was cannon fire again early today on the Western Front'.

It was a cold, hard winter, and life in blacked-out Fécamp was far from gay. The hours of work were long, and when they were over there was nothing to do except write letters or go drinking with colleagues or with some of the British troops who were billeted just outside the town. They were in charge of a store of poison gas. It does not say much for their security arrangements that we all knew from casual conversation not only where the stuff was kept but also what it was made of and what its effects were.

After a few weeks, it was suggested that as the senior – in fact, the only – producer on the strength, I should accompany George Busby to Paris each week, to represent the creative staff at the meetings. I jumped at the idea.

The meetings, at which a dozen or so administrators were present, were routine affairs that were got over as quickly as possible. On one occasion somebody put forward the idea that a weekly programme should be broadcast giving the British troops a little gentle instruction about French habits and customs: in fact, why not go the whole hog and teach them a few words of French, as well? Obviously such a programme would have to be produced in Paris and, as it would give me an extra day or two in the capital every week, I supported the scheme wholeheartedly. Inevitably, it was proposed that a committee should be formed to advise me, and that the Comtesse de Fels, who was already taking a great interest in our work, should be invited to chair it.

One of the first things debated by the committee members, all of whom were titled or high up in the realms of government-supported culture, was what the programme should be called and, after endless discussion they opted for 'Tommy's Half Hour', which only French minds could have evolved and which, considering Tommy was supposed already to have thirteen hours of programmes a day dedicated to him, was a rather cynical title. The members were also prolific in ideas for items. I was presented with scripts entitled 'Stamp Collecting', 'A Tiger Hunt in Indo-China', 'Bird Song' and 'The Invention of the Turbine Engine'.

The heads of the Czech and Austrian units also attended the weekly Paris meetings. At one, the Austrian, Dr Bauer, reported that he had been receiving death threats. As an example, he produced an anonymous letter which read, '*Cochon Autrichien, tu seras mort avant la fin du mois. Heil Hitler*'.

As a reasonable precaution, it was proposed that a couple of the French soldiers, who were on permanent guard at both studio and transmitter, should be detailed to escort him through the blacked-out streets after his transmission, which finished at midnight. Bauer, a surprisingly young High Court judge from Vienna, pooh-poohed the idea: he had told nobody but us about the threats, and it was agreed that we should keep the matter secret from the rest of the station staff.

At the request of the engineers, the English announcers took it in turns to sit with the Czechs and Austrians during their transmissions. This was because it was feared that the shouting and table-thumping, which took place during angry denunciations of Hitler, would take the transmitter off the air. It was not a demanding occupation; it was just a matter of sitting at the control panel, reading a book and occasionally putting out a hand to turn down the volume if things became noisy.

A few nights after that Paris meeting, it was my turn. At midnight, Bauer and I said goodnight to the sentries and stepped out into the pitch dark street. There was no moon, and we had a ten-minute walk through the deserted town to our hotel in the Place Thiers. We chatted with studied nonchalance and did not quicken our pace, but I am sure

Bauer's thoughts were running on the same lines as mine: Will it be a knife or a bullet? From which doorway will the attack come? It also occurred to me, selfishly, that in the darkness it would be almost impossible for a prospective assassin to differentiate between Bauer and myself. I am happy to report that the attack never came.

At Christmas there was a lot of forced jollity. At a Christmas dinner at the Hotel de la Poste, with toasts and songs in English, Czech and German, we assured each other that we would all spend the following Christmas with our families, with the war over and Czechoslovakia and Austria liberated – although we did not speculate as to how all this would be brought about. Afterwards there was a dance at the studio. It was a sober party because the transmissions had to be kept going, and we were spelling each other in twos and threes. During the morning I had produced an elaborate programme called 'Christmas Cavalcade', with special material recorded in London by Sir Seymour Hicks, Bunny Austin, Alice Delysia, Christoper Stone, and many other celebrated people.

I was recording 'Tommy's Half Hour' every week at Poste Parisien, which was just like old times. During the afternoon of 3 January, George Busby came into the control cubicle, while I was recording, and told me that the protests of the military authorities had taken effect and that all transmissions from Fécamp were to stop at once.

So that was that! It would be at least six months before the new transmitter at Mantes would be completed, even if Shanks were able to continue his current successes in getting hold of equipment. Obviously we were all out of a job. George and I were joined by Godfrey Holloway, who was also in Paris, and the three of us went out for some morose drinking.

The next evening, after I had recorded some numbers by Josephine Baker, who sang with Wal-Berg's orchestra, Godfrey and I travelled together to Fécamp, where we found the

English staff holding a wake in the upstairs room of the Café des Colonnes.

For a few days, George Busby found everybody useless jobs to keep them occupied. Not having had a day off for over seven weeks, I was not sorry to take things easy. I spent a lot of time at a turntable, playing through some of the pre-war programmes I had produced in London. It was a morbid occupation and, sensibly, George asked me to stop. Not very patriotically, we had all adopted a German disc as our favourite background listening, Zarah Leander singing, 'Merci, mon ami, das ist wonderschon'.

Richard Meyer arrived from somewhere and interviewed each of us in turn, saying that for most of us it was the sack, but that he hoped we might be free to rejoin the station when, and if, it got going again. George Busby was to stay in Fécamp to look after the business affairs of the station, and our two engineers, Cliff Sandall and Timmy Timms, were to continue to keep the technical side in good shape. Dick told me there was a chance that 'Tommy's Half Hour' might be transmitted from Poste Parisien, where it could fulfil the two useful functions of keeping the Countess and the committee interested, and keeping the name Radio International on the air. He suggested that I stayed in Fécamp for the time being, to be on hand if I were wanted.

Reaction to the sack varied from man to man. It did not worry Ralph Hurcombe, because he was going to join the army anyway, but at the other end of the scale Bob Danvers-Walker moaned and wailed, and said how hard it was for a married man with two children to be thrown on the scrapheap after only seven years with the firm. In fact, he went back to London and immediately took a job as commentator for the Pathé newsreel, which he held until the concern packed up thirty years later.

Nobody could return to London immediately because there were many formalities to be gone through, not one of which, I am sure, hampered the German war effort in the very least. First, permission to leave the country had to be obtained, both from the military authorities and from the prefect of the department in Rouen. As the others were going through this rigmarole, I went along with them, so that I would not have to hang about if 'Tommy's Half Hour' fell through. The prefect was an affable old party who interviewed us *en bloc*, assured us that as we were virtually *functionaires* there would be no difficulties, and took ten francs from each of us. In exchange, our passports were graced with a full page of handwriting, two rubber-stamp imprints in violet ink, an adhesive fiscal stamp and a signature, which seemed to add up to a very good ten francs worth. To my disappointment, nobody wished to make any mark on my wartime *carte d'identité*, which I still keep as a curiosity; a long, green document with twelve folds in it, it contains not only my photograph, description and thumb-prints, but also forty-eight neat spaces for recording changes of address, each of which had to be certified by the commissariat of police at both ends.

One by one the members of the English staff left, and each departure was an occasion for a party. Charles Maxwell left his packing to the very last minute. When we went to his flat to help him we discovered that he had an extraordinarily comprehensive collection of French liqueurs, and that there was an inch or so remaining in each bottle. To go from one to another of those strong, sweet, sticky liquids is an alcoholic experience I do not wish to repeat.

They were gloomy days, and the only occasion that sticks out in my memory is the time when Timms and I were arrested as spies. Late one evening, we were sitting in the Café des Colonnes, which was deserted except for a singularly drunken British sergeant, whom we noticed to be staring at us glassily. After a time he got to his feet and lurched towards us, weaving from side to side and pointing a rifle. What he was doing, wandering round the pubs with a rifle, I can't imagine, but he had one and, if his finger was as unreliable as his legs, it was going off at any moment.

'I heard you!' he slurred. 'I heard you! You were talking English.'

'We are English,' I said. 'We're at the radio station. Er – join us for a drink.'

My attempts at friendliness did no good.

'You're spies, that's what you are – spies.'

It was obvious that somebody had been doing something to make the local British soldiery security-minded – and it was about time, too – but the effect the lectures had had on this fool was unfortunate. He told us that we were under arrest, and that he was going to take us to the army post opposite the abbey. That was fine so far as we were concerned; what we were worrying about was that wavering rifle muzzle.

As we went out into the street, he said – I know this sounds far-fetched, but it is true – 'You two walk in front, and if I try to run away, you shoot me.'

It was a nerve-racking walk down to the army post, where the sergeant's mates took his rifle away and put him to bed. They were kind enough to give us a much-needed drink.

Eventually George Busby, the two engineers, Beryl Muir and I were the only ones left in a wintry Fécamp. The weather was awful, and I seemed to have a perpetual cold. A laundry list which has unaccountably survived lists four shirts, two sets of underwear, six pairs of socks and seventeen handkerchieves. A visit to a cinema was the only excitement, and all three of them seemed to show nothing but noisy farces. On 20 January I celebrated my birthday with an outing to Le Havre, and a few days later the long-awaited telegram arrived, 'Send Plomley Paris'. For some reason, I had to take a lot of records and office equipment with me, and I remember setting off for the station in the early-morning darkness with a fat porter from the Hotel Canchy pushing a handcart piled high with the stuff.

For diplomatic reasons, George Shanks had taken a flat in the same Boulevard Raspail block in which his chief political contact, Max Brousset, who was *chef de cabinet* to George

Mandel, lived. It was a handsome seventh-floor flat, with a roof garden embellished with statuary which he had looted from the gardens of the Mantes château. He was sharing the flat with a young English friend, Richard Baines, who had been with us for a while in Fécamp. Shanks told me that, as an economy, we would give up the office in the Poste Parisien building and use a room in the flat: he also said that the restarting of 'Tommy's Half Hour' was by no means certain, but that there was no harm in my getting some material ready. I could also start work on preparing programme schedules for the July reopening of Radio International.

The first job was to clear the Poste Parisien office. The library of some thousands of discs was moved down to the Boulevard Raspail, but all those which had been specially recorded for broadcasting must, for copyright reasons, be destroyed. I spent a melancholy few hours breaking across my knee recordings of programmes which had been part of my life since I had started work in radio.

For three years, until the war started, the French government had been steadily devaluing the franc, until it now stood at 176 to the pound. This gave a wonderful advantage to the British. Sometimes I used to take my elevenses at the Café du Colisée, a superior establishment in the Avenue des Champs Elysées, where a champagne cocktail, served with a small red caviar sandwich, could be had for ninepence, which was also the price of a modest meal at a small restaurant. A bottle of *vin de table*, bought from a grocer's shop cost only three-halfpence, and I remember buying a good seat at the Opera to see *The Magic Flute* for twelve francs, which was less than one-and-threepence. For years, I had worn only silk shirts and pyjamas, which cost very little more than cotton ones did in England.

The Countess had lined up some musical members of distinguished French families for me to audition, and I listened dutifully to drawing-room sopranos and 17-year-old violin students. She also asked me if I would be interested

YOU ARE ON THE AIR

LISTEN IN TO RADIO NORMANDY
on SUNDAY at **10** p.m. (**212·6** METRES)

Announcing a broadcast of the second tour of *Radio Normandy Calling*, from the stage of the Hippodrome, Eastbourne

Compering a Donald Peers programme in an IBC studio. Donald is leaning on the piano, which Arthur Young is playing

Radio International, January 1940. L. to r. David Davies (standing), Charles Maxwell, R.P.

Diana. My favourite picture of my wife *(Angus McBean)*

R.P. looking rather tired after a seven-day journey from Paris *(News-Chronicle)*

in some comedy material, as the daughter of a friend of hers collected English jokes. I assured her I would be delighted to see them. A few days later, a shy, pretty girl came to the office with her mother, who spoke very little English. Demurely, with downcast eyes, the girl presented me with a thick script consisting of handwritten jokes. I glanced down at them – they were filthy!

After a number of delays, 'Tommy's Half Hour' started its weekly run on Poste Parisien on Saturday afternoons. Each programme consisted of a few discs by popular British artists, a lighthearted French lesson in which a French woman instructed a young English soldier (played by a Cockney entertainer I found in a night club), an interview with an English-speaking celebrity, and a musical contribution by a celebrated French star. If any Tommies ever happened to hear it, I think they might well have enjoyed it.

One day, Shanks told me he had met Noël Coward, who was in Paris, and that he thought he might be able to persuade him to come to the studio to record an interview that afternoon. It happened to be a wet day. I had left home in a pair of very old shoes which had almost disintegrated in the rain, and I thought that I would feel at a disadvantage in interviewing a man who was always so singularly well dressed, so I dashed out and bought a new pair. Because I had very little time I bought a pair which was too small. I waited about, but Mr Coward did not materialize. That was disappointing at the time but quite understandable in the light of later revelations, because it was Coward who, angry at the way Radio International had been breaking all the rules, had spearheaded the attack to have the station taken off the air. I regretted having bought the shoes.

An interviewee who did materialize was André Maurois, who was brought along by Richard Meyer. A quiet, friendly man in his fifties, wearing military uniform, his English was impeccable – after all, he had been an interpreter with the British forces during the 1914–18 war and had written biographies of Shelley, Byron and Disraeli, as well as a history of England. He spoke a sensible piece about Anglo-French friendship. As a token of gratitude, Meyer gave him a small portable radio which could be slung over his shoulder on a strap. I have often wondered what that set was, and who made it, and where Meyer got it, because at that time a so-called portable receiver was a large contraption at least the size of a portable gramophone, whereas this model was barely larger than a small modern transistor set.

One of the Countess's activities was the organization of an Anglo-French charity gala at the Opera. The President of the Republic was to be there, and the Duke of Windsor, the British Ambassador, Reynaud, Deladier, Barraut, *et tout le gratin*. The stage setting was to be an improvised troop theatre somewhere up near the front, and every available French and British star was to be roped in to take part. The producer was to be Paul Colline, who would also compere. Being mobilized, Lieutenant Colline would appear in uniform.

It was then decided that, as there would be many British in the audience, there should be an English-speaking compere as well. I was asked to do the job and, to match Colline, to wear a British Army uniform. There was no difficulty in borrowing one, because I knew a sergeant at the British Leave Club in the Place de la République who could supply anything. He had once been manager of the Grand Theatre, Clapham, and he used to sell me an occasional bottle of duty-free gin at an advantageous price.

The rehearsal was averagely chaotic. The French were fielding Maurice Chevalier, Bordas and some assorted dancers and conjurers, while our side included Gracie Fields, Jack Warner, Richard Murdoch and Jack Hylton and his Orchestra. Hylton was just about to branch out as an impresario, and he afterwards pinched the presentation and troop theatre setting for his stage production of *Garrison Theatre*, which he presented at the London Palladium.

There was an outbreak of tantrums because Paul Colline

had written some rhymed couplets to introduce each of the artists, including the British ones, but Jack Hylton said that his section of the programme, which also included the performances of Monsieur Warner and Monsieur Murdoch, had already been rehearsed and agreed with the BBC, who were broadcasting it, and he did not want any French announcements, whether in rhymed couplets or not. He did not want my services either, but I could not have cared less.

As the audience entered the auditorium, the curtain was already up, and they saw French and British soldiers erecting their improvised theatre. When the audience was settled, Colline and I entered and said, he in rhymed French couplets and I in less formal English, that the tradition of the punctuality of kings had been passed on to presidents of republics, and some smart stage management in the front of the house had M. Lebrun appear in his box immediately his name was mentioned.

The show went well. I had quite a busy evening, nipping on and introducing artists, and ad-libbing with Aimé Simon-Girard, who was doing a mock radio commentary from one of the boxes.

Towards the end of the performance, the wings began to fill up with high-ranking French officers. Obviously word was getting round in military circles that the show was on and that, being a military occasion, it would be difficult to refuse admission to brasshats. It has always been every Frenchman's dream to get backstage at the Opera, because of the ballet girls. That we had a minimum of ballet girls on this occasion, they were not to know, and anyway they came on spec. The crush in the wings was getting so bad that artists, including me, were finding it difficult to get on and off the stage. Once, I heard my cue coming up, but my way was blocked by a general. There was only one thing to do, and I did it — I pushed him out of the way. The reaction of this French general at being pushed by someone he presumed to be a British private was fascinating: he went bright red and swelled up, like an angry fish in a Walt

Disney cartoon. I thought it expedient to make my exit on the other side.

Before leaving London I had become engaged to a young and beautiful Chinese actress named Diana Wong, and I had been pulling strings to try to get permission for her to join me in Paris. Eventually I was successful, and I met her at Le Bourget, finding her rather shaken after a flight in an aircraft with boarded-up windows. We took a flat on the Left Bank, just at the foot of the Rue de la Montagne de Ste Geneviève, in a splendidly picturesque and cosmopolitan quarter and our lives quickly took on a pleasant routine: I would work in the Boulevard Raspail office or make recordings, while Diana took French lessons, did the marketing and embarked on some rather tentative cooking. We made plans to be married by our friend the Rev. Donald Caskie, Pastor of the Church of Scotland in Paris, who was later to achieve fame for his exploits as 'The Kilted Pimpernel'.

One day, I received a letter from Jack Hargreaves. The great jazz success in London was the Hatchett's Swingtette, which Arthur Young was leading at that celebrated Piccadilly establishment. Jack had been appointed entertainments manager of the St Regis Hotel, in Cork Street, and he was setting up a jazz group, featuring Harry Parry and George Shearing, in opposition – and could I find Django Reinhardt and find out how much money he would require to go and play in London?

I asked around and discovered that Django was playing in a small group at a rather undistinguished Left Bank nightclub called Le Jockey. Diana and I went along. During an interval between sets, I crossed to the tiny bandstand. 'How about London, Django?' I asked. 'You'd be with a good group, and Stephane Grappelli's over there, so you'd be able to record together. You'd make much more money than you can here.'

He was not interested. Paris was his home, and money was not all that important.

In fact, the St Regis was to be an early casualty in the

Blitz, but there would have been plenty of work for him throughout the war and, remembering the contribution made by Stephane Grappelli's violin to what little gaiety there was in wartime London, it would have been great to have Django's guitar as well. Perhaps I was not a good enough salesman.

In April, the Germans invaded Norway and Denmark, but those countries seemed a long way away and even when, the following month, they sailed through Holland and Belgium and came on to French territory – well, that had happened in the First War, and they had been pushed back again. The truth was that Diana and I were much too busy living our own lives to take much notice of larger issues. True, there were air raid alerts at night and enemy planes flying over, but the radio and newspapers were reassuring. In fact, they revealed little of what was going on, and news was often several days out of date before it was released. Angry editors put their papers on the streets leaving as white space the columns which the censors had deleted.

Edward Stirling, who had run his English theatre troupe in Paris and other European cities for many years, invited me to play Antonio in the trial scene from *The Merchant of Venice*, which he proposed to tour round schools near Paris. But we had only one or two rehearsals before the project ran out of steam. I think the first time I realized that things might be serious was when, on 21 May, I walked into the radio station, Radio Cité, and asked to book a channel to dub some American dance music on to slow speed discs for eventual use at Mantes. The taking of Arras and Amiens had just been announced, and the staff were amazed that I could be bothered with such a project at such a time, and regretted that they could not help me. It was also disturbing, when visiting the Ministère des Affaires Etrangères, to see men with wheelbarrows piling the archives onto enormous bonfires burning all over the lawn.

One day I was in a little English bar near the Etoile when the news came through that the Germans had entered

Forges-les-Eaux. An elderly Englishman standing beside me said, 'Ridiculous! They can't have. I go there for weekends.'

I gradually became aware that most of the familiar British faces to be seen around Paris were no longer visible. I assumed they had left, and was amused and scornful. For heaven's sake, whatever could go wrong in Paris?

On the evening of Sunday 9 June, Diana and I ran into some American friends on a Metro platform. With them was the English writer, Rupert Downing, and I joked with him that we must be the only Britons left in Paris. As a matter of fact, we were nearly right.

8

It was by good luck and a few minor miracles that Diana and I did not spend the next four years in Fresnes prison.

During that Sunday night, there was some banging about from the anti-aircraft guns in the Luxembourg Gardens, but no alert was sounded. The following morning was fine and sunny.

The news on the radio was noncommittal. Apart from news bulletins, nothing was being broadcast except a monotonous interval signal of a phrase from 'La Marseillaise' played without expression on brass instruments, with a three-beat pause between each repetition . . . 'Aux armes, citoyens' – two – three – four . . . 'Aux armes, citoyens' – two – three – four . . . 'Aux armes, citoyens' . . .

I left for the office early. In the streets, there were the usual cars packed with refugees and luggage, making for the southern gates of the city, and the increasing number of military vehicles showed that Paris was well within the war zone. Some of the vehicles were crammed with weary and seemingly battle-worn troops.

At 28 Boulevard Raspail the lift was out of order, and I walked seven flights up the back stairs. As I reached the service balcony, I saw Jeanne Gastaud, the secretary, and Fernand, the office boy, leaning out of the window, looking very dejected indeed. Possibly I overdid my cheerful good mornings. They were in sole possession, as Dick Baines was in

Nantes working with an American Aid to Refugees unit, and George Shanks had gone to spend a few days with him. I sat down and began preparing some scripts of 'Tommy's Quarter Hour', a cut-down version of the programme which we hoped would be broadcast from Radio Méditerranée.

In the middle of the morning, the telephone rang, and Jeanne Gastaud answered it. She replied '*Oui*' a couple of times, and then hung up. She had gone rather pale. It had been Brousset, speaking from his office at the Ministry of the Interior. He had told her, tersely, to close the window shutters, turn off the gas and electricity and be prepared to vacate the office immediately: then he had replaced the receiver.

From Brousset, such curious behaviour was not unusual; he was inclined to get into flaps, and also he loved making mysteries of things. I suggested to Mlle Gastaud that she had better do as he had asked, and then try to reach him again in a few minutes. My own view, which I did not express, was that he had advance news of an impending air-raid and was warning us to be ready to dive down to the basement if things looked dangerous. He had previously told us that an advance tip-off by a captured fifth-columnist one morning the previous week had enabled French fighters to head off a large force of Luftwaffe bombers a hundred miles from the capital.

It took Jeanne Gastaud a long time to get him back on the line. When she succeeded, he gave her rapid instructions to close the office; she and Fernand were to call on him at the Ministry at 2.20, and they should make plans to leave Paris at once. I tried to get to the telephone to talk to him myself, but he had hung up. He had said nothing about me, which was not surprising, as my programme work hardly came into Brousset's sphere.

I went home to tell Diana to stand by for a move: perhaps she had better start packing. Then I went to the Ministry. There was a crowd in the anteroom, including a number of journalists and a Japanese diplomat. Nobody spoke except in whispers. I joined Jeanne Gastaud and Fernand on a red-plush settee. One of their worries was getting some money, as they had two weeks wages due to them. Fernand told me he was 18, and due to be called-up in a few months: he was an orphan, with no responsibilities, and would probably go south and volunteer. Jeanne Gastaud had an invalid mother to look after, but she possessed dual nationality and held an American passport.

After some minutes, Georges Mandel walked through the room to his office, looking neither to left nor right. He was wearing a perfectly fitting morning coat, and his linen was impeccably white. He looked calm and confident, and this small, immaculate Jew was the most stable person I was to see for days.

There was a stream of people in and out of Brousset's room: eventually we were all three shown in together. Brousset did not reflect the confidence of his chief; he was flabby and perspiring, and incessantly jumping up from his chair and collapsing into it again. He shook us by the hands and disposed of us speedily. He formally sacked Jeanne Gastaud and Fernand, and regretted that he had no money for them: he told me that he had had no word from Shanks. Things were very bad − desperate. We must go at once. Where? He shrugged. We must make our own arrangements. I said something about staying in Paris until the government left. He told me the government had already gone, except Mandel and his staff. They were leaving that night − it was all very secret.

I walked with the others as far as the Avenue des Champs Elysées, then went down to the British Railways office near the Place de l'Opéra. It was full of British subjects, but the staff could do nothing to help them: all the northern passenger ports were in enemy hands, and only St Malo was still open. They had no information as to sailings and could not supply tickets; intending passengers must make their own way and take their chance. I looked on at all this with a rather superior attitude. There could not possibly be all that hurry. After all, I had been given a government tip-off which should put me twenty-four hours ahead of any real, serious panic. In any case, I did not want to go back to England: I would join Shanks and

Dick in Nantes for a few days, until the trouble blew over, and then come back to Paris and take up my job where I had left it. A few days in the west would be pleasant.

Having settled this in my mind, I walked down to the Gare Montparnasse to book a couple of seats on the evening train – just like that! It was when I came in sight of the station that I realized what the score was. As far as the eye could see there were refugees, crowded in the vast forecourt, camping on the pavements – with bundles, birdcages, prams, bath tubs, poultry, babies, dogs. A cordon was drawn up round the station, and no more tickets were being issued that day. I managed to get inside and walked round for a few minutes, looking at the tragic, fascinating scene. Tears, sobs, curses, apathy, stupidity, age, youth, riches, poverty, thousands of people with all that remained of their homes under their arms. I was told that the booking office would probably open again at six o'clock the next morning. I went home to report to Diana, stopping at the office on the way to pick up a few papers and personal belongings.

Despite what I had seen, some incredible idiocy, or it may have been habit or it may have been obstinacy, decided me to take some of our possessions with us – and we had plenty of possessions, because Diana had imported the whole of her extensive wardrobe. We looked through all our belongings, tagging everything in one of three categories: must take, take if possible and leave behind. By far the greatest amount seemed to be in the must take category.

I left Diana to cope with the packing, and went back to the Gare Montparnasse to see what the chances were of buying places in a car. They were nil. I trudged round the surrounding streets, speaking to the drivers of cars or lorries, but either they had no petrol or no permit to leave the city. At one moment, a murmur ran through the crowd: it had been announced on the radio that Italy had declared war on France – a cowardly stab in the back. A German plane flew high overhead, and a solitary AA gun barked at it with hopeless inaccuracy. I went home again to help with the packing.

It was hot, and we broke off to go down to the corner café for shandy. It was a rough and noisy place, and one that ordinarily we did not use, but tonight everyone was quiet, and there seemed a strange telepathic bond of mutual sympathy. We still did not like to admit that we were running away, and I told the concierge that my office had been moved to the west for a while, and that I would be away only a short time. He helped me to move down to the basement the luggage we were leaving behind – a heavy cabin trunk, a radio, a gramophone and records, some books and kitchen utensils. That still left, to take with us, four large suitcases, one small suitcase, a hat box, a despatch case and a parcel of food. We must have been crazy. In one of the large suitcases, I had packed a pile of slow-speed discs of programmes I had been recording: what for, I cannot imagine. On all the cases, I painted 'PLOMLEY, à NANTES' in white paint.

We planned to get to the Gare Montparnasse soon after four o'clock, and I went out at 3.30 to try to find a taxi. I walked round the Latin Quarter, crossed to the Ile de la Cité, where Notre Dame looked squarely set for another thousand years, and then walked through Les Halles. Already, a stream of cars was heading southwest, with mattresses tied to the roofs as a slender protection against machine-gun bullets. Over the city was a thick, smokey haze, which I had noticed settling the evening before, and it made the dawn very lovely.

For an hour and three-quarters, I tramped the streets vainly, and then had the idea of going along the *quai* to the Gare d'Orsay, which was still open for trains going due south as far as Orléans. There I found a taxi, but it was nearly 5.30 when I got back to the flat. The concierge and his wife were up to say goodbye. We loaded our foolish luggage and set off. The crowds at the Gare Montparnasse seemed even greater than on the previous day. We drove round to the back, where families were struggling with their bags and bundles up a long, cobbled slope which led to the station concourse. The taxi-driver turned out us and our luggage into the middle of the road and went off in search of another fare. We tried to handle the bags by ourselves, but there were too many of them and they were too heavy, and moving them two at a time took too long. I left Diana in charge while I went to prospect. I found an old woman pushing her luggage up the slope on an iron station trolley which was too heavy for her, and I helped her to the top and took over the trolley. When we had got our belongings up into the station, Diana left me to join a queue for tickets, while I waited in an interminable line to register the bags. Everyone's face was streaked with black, like a chimney-sweep's, and it was obvious that the sun was not going to break through the haze. There was a theory that it was a smoke-screen put up as a defence against bombing, while others said that it was smoke drifting from Senlis and Compiègne, which were in flames: in fact, as we learned later, it came from the burning of oil storage tanks down the Seine.

I had been told the day before that a train for Nantes was due out at about 8.20. Diana came back with tickets just before 8 o'clock, when I was only about a quarter of the way up the baggage queue. I persuaded her to go and squeeze onto the train, and I would follow as soon as I could. Once she got to Nantes, she was to meet all trains from Paris. She took a lot of persuading but she finally went. I knew I was taking a risk and that the line might be cut at any minute, but I hadn't the heart to abandon the majority of our worldly belongings on the station. I was already mourning the loss of a half-bottle of whisky, which I had dropped.

I stayed in line until nearly ten o'clock and finally registered all the baggage, except a despatch case to which was strapped my overcoat. Such was my blithe innocence that I asked whether the bags would reach Nantes that night, which raised a laugh.

I now had a ticket for Nantes, was unburdened, and was hungry, so I decided to leave the station to get something to eat, relying on my ticket to get me back in again. I breakfasted in a café, and then realized that I had not had my *carte d'identité* stamped with permission to leave Paris. It seemed important to keep my papers in order, so I went down on the packed

188

Metro to the commissariat of the fifth *arrondissement*. There, they were busy dealing with a flood of unhappy Italians who had suddenly become enemy aliens, and I was waved away. On my way back to the Metro I found my usual difficulty in passing bookstalls, and stopped, on the Quai and in the Boulevard St Michel, to buy a back number of '*Les Oeuvres Libres*', containing the text of Pierre Löuys's verse comedy, '*Les Aventures du Roi Pausole*', a pacifist book in English, and a film magazine dating back to silent days.

When I got back to the Gare Montparnasse, I realized my incredible idiocy in having left the place. The crowds were even thicker, an armed cordon again surrounded the station, and I quickly discovered that my ticket to Nantes, my British passport, and my official identity papers were equally useless in getting me back inside. I began to circle the building, pleading and cajoling without success. At last, at one entrance, seeing the attention of the guards distracted by an incident in the crowd, I tried to slip through, but was hauled back and interrogated by a senior police officer, who demanded to know if I were a Pole. I produced all my papers and talked fast, and proved that I was not whoever he thought I was. To my intense relief I was passed through.

Having got back inside, I could see no immediate advantage: there was no sign of any train and the crowd was so dense that I could hardly move. I sat down on the ground and waited to see what happened next. At about 12.30, a voice on the public address system announced that no more trains would be leaving that day or until further notice. Wails and lamentations went up from the crowd. The announcement could only mean that the line to the west had been cut.

All I could do was resign myself to having to hitch-hike somehow to Nantes, and heaven only knew how long that would take. I decided to stay in the station for the time being on the off-chance of being able to get a local train, perhaps as far as Versailles, which would be, at any rate, a few kilometres on my way. After a time, I got talking to a porter, who told me that a train was standing at a subsidiary platform some way down the line, but nobody knew if, when or where it was going. I picked up my despatch case and overcoat and started walking down the track. As I came out of the station, I could look down on massed crowds in the streets below. From a police loudspeaker van came an amplified voice, repeating over and over again, *'Il n'y a plus de trains. Rentrez chez vous. Soyez calme. Rentrez chez vous.'*

I came to a couple of bare concrete platforms, rather like the ones which used to be outside Twickenham station for the use of rugby football crowds on match days, and at them were two trains. They were already crammed as full as trains possibly could be, but I ran up and down them, hoping to find just an inch or two of space. There was one coach which was not quite so tightly packed as the others: it was a first-class coach and, although the train was obviously *déclassé*, there seemed among some of these sad, bewildered people an idea that such luxury was not for them. With much shoving and grunting, I heaved myself into the corridor and stood there, wedged solidly.

By now, word had got round in the main station that the trains were there, and crowds were running and stumbling down the track towards us. It was a sight that did not seem possible in real life; this could only happen in a film. New arrivals tried to climb through the windows, or to lift babies or disabled people through, but there was an obvious limit to the amount of humanity the trains could contain, and then the crowds could only stand silent and defeated, staring at us lucky ones who were aboard.

We stayed there, in the heat of the afternoon, for some hours, and then began to move, very slowly, stopping and starting. From time to time, the track ran near roads, crammed with cars and slow-moving farm carts and pedestrians – an endless procession of misery. There were isolated army units, too – artillery, or armoured vehicles, or infantry. Nobody knew where we were bound for, but we were on the main line westwards, and that was in the right direction.

Through the long, hot afternoon and evening, the train

laboriously probed its way. At every halt, passengers climbed down onto the track to relieve themselves, hurrying to force their way back into the sweating mass on board. At dusk, we stopped for a long time, while flashes lit the skyline. Guns? – but it was to the north, so it was more likely to be bombs. But there was no sound, no vibration, so it might have been some electrical manifestation.

It was well after 2.00 am when we eventually and miraculously reached Nantes, and disentangled ourselves to leave the train. There was not an inch of space in the darkened station; refugees were huddled everywhere. How was I to find Diana in this chaos? I groped my way round, looking into the shadows, peering into sleeping faces. Luckily, Diana is easily identifiable, and I began to ask every railway official I could find, '*Une jeune chinoise – Avez-vous vu une jeune chinoise?*' At last, I found a man who had a scrap of crumpled paper with an address on it – there had been a young Chinese girl, in tears: she had been taken away by the Red Cross.

I pushed my way out of the station, with the piece of paper in my hand. Of all things, I found a taxi, drawn up outside as if it were peacetime, and the driver there to meet business men back on the late train from the capital. He drove me to an address in the Avenue de Launay, where the door was opened by a young man named Pierre Bertho, who had filled his little house with refugees. He fetched Diana, who had never expected to see me again. Speaking little French, with only a little money, and bemused by the crowds around her, she had waited for hours in the dark station, until it had been announced that there would be no more trains from Paris. Room was made for me on the floor of the attic which she was sharing with many others.

In the morning we thanked our host and went out into the streets. We were 240 miles west of Paris; surely life could continue normally here – we would find a hotel room, and wait until the situation clarified. We trailed round the city, trying every hotel from the grandest to the crumbiest; we asked in every café; we stopped people in the street. There were thousands doing exactly what we were doing: there was no accommodation of any sort anywhere. We enquired for George Shanks and Dick Baines at the address I had from the Paris office, but were told that they had moved to Les Sables d'Olonne, sixty miles to the south. We decided to go after them the next day, in the hope of being able to make plans, or at least to borrow some money, because our supply was perilously small. We went to the station to enquire whether our luggage had arrived, but of course it hadn't, and what on earth we could have done with it if it had, I can't imagine.

Darkness fell, and we were still looking for somewhere to spend the night. We were in a residential quarter of the town when the air raid sirens wailed. There was a slamming of doors and a hurrying for cover: air raid warnings were taken seriously in this estuary port. We asked an old man to direct us to a shelter, and he told us to go with him. He took us down into a crowded cellar, and presently the earth shook with distant reverberations. When the all-clear sounded, Diana was in an exhausted sleep. It was a job to wake her. I asked if we might sleep the night in the cellar. A kind Madame Monnier, hearing that we were homeless, took us to her house in the Rue Cresset. She gave us a room, and Diana went exploring to find the bathroom. Carelessly, she put on a light when the window was not curtained, and there was a blowing of whistles and shouted threats from an air raid warden in the courtyard below that he would have Madame Monnier summonsed. We felt guilty and, in the morning, we spent some of our remaining store of francs in sending her some roses.

We went in search of the public baths, and found that Nantes provides the most civilized amenities in this direction. Where else would you find a double bathroom? Yes, they had one with two baths for two people, and what an excellent idea. Why should a bath always be a solitary occasion instead of a social one?

Then we went down the coast to Les Sables d'Olonne by train, which took nearly six hours. George Shanks was not there, but we found Dick, who was working at a *centre d'acceuil* for refugees. Generously, he lent us a thousand francs, and found us accommodation for the night in an attic room in an hotel. Leaning out of the dormer window and looking down into the narrow street, I could see a knot of people clustering at the door of a café. They were listening to a radio speech by Premier Reynaud, whose voice came up to us clearly. *'L'âme de la France n'est pas vaincue . . . Faut-il désespérer? Certes non . . . . nous gardons au coeur l'espérance.'* He was speaking from Tours. That night, while we slept, the Germans entered Paris.

I was out early the next morning. I called on Dick, and then went for a walk on the huge expanse of firm sand which gives the town its name. It was a glorious summer morning, and this was the kind of place in which one should be on holiday, to swim and laze and make love.

We went back to Nantes by bus, an easier journey. There was no news, but a lot of rumour, and there was no doubt that the situation was getting worse hour by hour. It seemed time to go to the British Consul to ask for some advice. When we found the British Consulate, it was shut — firmly and permanently shut.

So the British Consul had skipped. What was the next move? We went into a restaurant to have lunch and to think it over. It was a large, bare, basic restaurant, and it was crowded. Further down the room were half a dozen young privates in the Royal Army Pay Corps, who were eyeing Diana appreciatively. One of them, in fact, was eyeing her so exclusively that he failed to recognize me, and I had been at school with him. His name was Bayliss and I had known him quite well. I went over and spoke to him, and signed to Diana to come and join us. His unit had been moving progressively westward for weeks, and he assumed the next move would be out of the country. I told him of our situation. He nodded. 'We've heard that the British Consul's run away,' he said. 'The form is to go and see the American Consul.' We said thank you, and went in search of him.

The American Consul was a good man, and very helpful. 'You've two alternatives,' he said. 'They'll take you off from St

Nazaire, down the river, or there's a ship coming into St Malo on Sunday to evacuate British civilians. Take your choice.'

'Is it really as bad as that?' I asked. 'I don't want to leave France unless it's necessary.'

'It's up to you,' he said, 'but it looks pretty bad to me.'

Outside on the pavement, Diana and I looked at each other. St Nazaire was near – only twenty-eight miles away – while St Malo was four times as far and a cross-country journey, but I knew and loved St Malo, and I liked the idea of seeing it again and showing it to Diana. That sentimental decision almost certainly saved our lives: if we had gone to St Nazaire, we would have embarked on the *Lancastria*, which was bombed in the estuary and went down with an estimated 3,000 Britons on board. Among them was Bayliss.

Still obsessed by our luggage, we bought gum, labels and a blue pencil, and went to the station to re-mark our bags. Of course, they were not there, so we resigned ourselves to ditching them. At about five o'clock, we boarded a train going north. It was not terribly crowded. Soon after dark, however, we were made to change into a train that was hell on wheels. We sat on the floor. Sleep was impossible. The train crawled along.

At daybreak – it was now Saturday, and we had left Paris on Tuesday – everyone began climbing down at the frequent stops, to pick fruit from the trees or fetch water. We passed many trains of goods wagons filled with refugees. The inhabitants of one truck told us they were from Fécamp, and they must have been many days on the way, helplessly shunted about the northwestern railway system, and going God knew where. Outside Rennes, the train seemed to have come to a permanent stop, so we decided to walk along the track to the station.

We were told there would be a long wait before there was any chance of a train to St Malo. We had breakfast, and risked leaving the station to see if there was any other transport. It was hopeless; the town was packed with refugees, sitting miserably on the pavements. It was here that we saw the saddest sight of our exodus: at the approach to the station was a long, wooden fence, which was completely covered with thousands of pathetic, pinned-up messages for missing members of families.

Standing on the platform at Rennes Station, I experienced a strange coincidence. There had been a weekly paper called *Radio Pictorial*, which had existed until the outbreak of war. It was a glossy fan paper, full of photographs of radio stars, chatty gossip, recipes, fashion notes and rubbishy fiction with a radio studio background; and its main reason for existence was that it printed the Radio Normandy and Radio Luxembourg programmes. I had had a copy on my desk all the time I had worked in radio. Now, on my way out of France and on my way out of the whole commercial radio set-up, I saw its familiar bright orange cover lying between the rails. It was the only copy I had ever seen in France, except in our own studios. What curious chain of circumstances had brought it there? – but then what curious chain of circumstances had brought me there to see it?

The next leg of the journey was not too bad. In the train, we started to eat some cherries we had bought. A young girl eyed them hungrily, and I gave her a handful. She did not eat one until she had carefully shared them among the members of her family.

We reached St Malo at about five o'clock: it had taken us more than twenty-two hours to cover the 110 miles from Rennes. We had arrived in another world. Sunshine lay on the sleepy life of the old walled town, which appeared just as I had last seen it, apparently untouched by war. We took a horse cab from the station, and booked in at the large comfortable Hotel du Centre et de la Paix, where there was plenty of room and where they appeared delighted to see us.

We went to see the British Consul, who was still at his post, still in full control of the situation, and who assured us that a ship would be coming in for British civilians the next day. We bought some sorely needed clean linen.

While Diana was at the hotel, washing and mending her

clothes, and doing all the feminine chores she had had no chance to do for so many days, I walked down to the port, where I saw British troops being embarked on transports and more or less anything that would float: there was also a hospital ship which was being loaded. I did not like the look of things, because the Germans must have known very well what was going on, and surely it could not be long before the Luftwaffe began to take an interest in this not-so-miniature Dunkirk. I went into a *tabac* to buy some cigarettes, and the proprietor asked me if I were English. When I said I was, he sneered and said, 'The English are all running away.'

That evening, we found a quiet restaurant and, as it seemed we no longer had to conserve our French money, we ate an excellent, leisurely meal of lobster. Before going to bed, I wrote a rather hopeless letter to the station master at Nantes, asking him to hold our luggage, when it arrived, until he received further instructions.

We slept like logs in calm holiday rooms, in soft white beds. After breakfast we went out to buy food and drink, because we had been advised to take supplies for two days. I also went to the commissariat to have my *carte d'identité* stamped to show that I had officially arrived in St Malo. The morning's rumours included one that Russia had entered the war on the Allied side, and another that forty fifth-columnists had been shot in the town.

There were no taxis, and we had the help of a surly hotel porter with our pitiful collection of belongings, which now consisted of Diana's small weekend case, my despatch case, full of books and papers, with my overcoat still tied to it, a cardboard box containing six of Diana's hats, a canvas bag stuffed with food and a couple of bottles of wine, and a brown paper parcel of the dirty linen we had discarded so thankfully the evening before. The porter demanded a ridiculously high sum for his help.

The scene at the quay was, to say the least, animated. Britons from every part of France, Italy and the Low Countries were wrestling with luggage. Nobody was to be allowed on board until innumerable formalities had been completed, and there seemed a dozen queues to be joined for tickets, visas, passport stamps, embarkation cards, consulate clearance, customs, and what have you. The heat, the noise and the confusion were stunning, and there looked to be three times as many people on the quay as could ever hope to get into the ship, which I recognized as one of the Southern Railway craft usually on the Southampton–Le Havre crossing.

Towards mid-afternoon, every imaginable formality had been complied with, and we were all herded into a large shed. Diana and I retreated into a corner, on the side nearest the dock, and began to eat bread and butter and pâté: then, a section of the wall behind us was wheeled away, and we found ourselves right next to the gangway. Because of our advantageous position, we were almost the first aboard, so that we were able to commandeer bunks and deckchairs.

Once the civilians had been embarked, troops were packed aboard. The long, hot day dragged on. It was rumoured that we were waiting to join a convoy. Why no German plane appeared to bomb this sitting military target, I cannot imagine. That the situation was not entirely unobserved was evidenced by the occasional barking of a naval pom-pom gun in the distance.

I discovered that the officer in charge of the troops was a friend of mine, Joslyn Mainprice, who had been an announcer for the English commercial programmes from Radio Toulouse, and afterwards a frequent visitor to the Dover Castle. How it came about that a subaltern was senior officer aboard, and in command of so many men, I do not know, but Lieutenant Mainprice, whom I had known as a gentle, quiet-voiced man, had become a commanding, swashbuckling figure, with a Bren gun slung on his shoulder and a bottle of rum in his pocket. He told me his unit had had a rough time. Laconically, he described how he had killed a German parachutist who was holding him at gun point, by pretending to mop his brow, and then whisking off his steel helmet to smash it hard across the

German's neck. He had commandeered the saloon below to house his wounded.

After darkness fell the ship moved slowly out of harbour. There was no sign of a convoy nor of any other craft. Diana went below to her bunk quite early, while I stayed on the crowded deck with Joslyn and drank rum. His sergeant-major came up to him, saluted and said, 'Smith has just died, sir.'

'Then throw him overboard,' said Joslyn. 'I'm not filling up any forms.'

Later in the crossing, I observed that same sergeant-major making enthusiastic love to a girl in a deckchair, while a superior lady was saying, 'That's my maid, and I've never known her behave like this before.'

Off Jersey the ship hove to and light signals were exchanged: then the engines were started again and we continued on our way. Peacefully, at midday, we sailed up Southampton Water. The familiar sight of a British policeman's helmet has never struck me as comical, but when Diana and I saw a policeman on the quay below us, we both began to giggle, rather hysterically.

A few days later a bill came through the letter box. It was from the Southern Railway and requested payment for two passages from St Malo to Southampton on 16/17 June.

Having been home to see my parents, who had received none of the mail I had despatched to them for several weeks, and who had, understandably, been exceedingly worried, my first call was at the IBC. I remembered to return the two stop watches belonging to the firm which I had been carrying in my pockets for the past eight days: I suppose I had salvaged them as the tools of my trade.

It was strange to be in the Portland Place building with so few people about: all my friends had left, and there was only a small administrative staff to keep things ticking over. When Captain Leonard Plugge heard of my arrival, he sent for me. It was the first time I had been in the supremo's office. I assumed that he wanted to congratulate me on my good fortune in getting back to England, or to ask for specific information about the situation in the Paris office when I had left, but his first question, in his usual high-pitched voice, was, 'Plomley, where's the French fleet?'

This rocked me back on my heels a little, because I was having difficulty in remembering exactly where I was myself. 'The French fleet is vital to us,' continued the honourable and gallant Member for Chatham, and he continued to look at me enquiringly. I could only reply that, although I had covered quite a lot of French territory during the past week or so, I did not remember having come across the fleet, whereupon he lost interest, and the interview came to an end.

A first consideration was to earn a little money because, having lived on a cut salary for the best part of a year, my resources were low. As a start, I sold the story of our escape to the *News Chronicle* for a few guineas, and told it on the BBC's 'The World Goes By' for a few more. I had a session with Richard Meyer to discuss the company's liability for the loss of my belongings, but I am no good at that sort of financial argy-bargy and, in any case, the company was in no way responsible for the loss of Diana's worldly goods. I came away with a month's salary plus a small sum which enabled us to buy a few necessary clothes.

Now, there had to be a fresh start: in which direction, I had no idea.

A few months later, I was to read in an evening paper that Joslyn Mainprice had shot himself in a bedroom at the Savoy Hotel. It would seem that the gentle, quiet-voiced Joslyn was the real one.

Index

Index